KNITTED SAFARI FRIENDS

KNITTED SAFARI FRIENDS

20 adorable animals to make

SARAH KEEN

CONTENTS

INTRODUCTION

It has been a happy time for me, making up these designs. All the usual animals are included in the collection of 20 safari friends. I hope you have enjoyment with whichever toys you decide to create.

ELEPHANT 16
HIPPO 24

LION 32
ZEBRA 38
TIGER 44

GIRAFFE 50
MONKEY 56

RHINO 62
FLAMINGO 76
ANTEATER 70

WEAVER BIRD 82
SLOTH 88

MEERKAT 94
BUFFALO 102
WARTHOG 108

GORILLA 116
PORCUPINE 122

ANTELOPE 128
CROCODILE 134
VULTURE 140

ELEPHANT

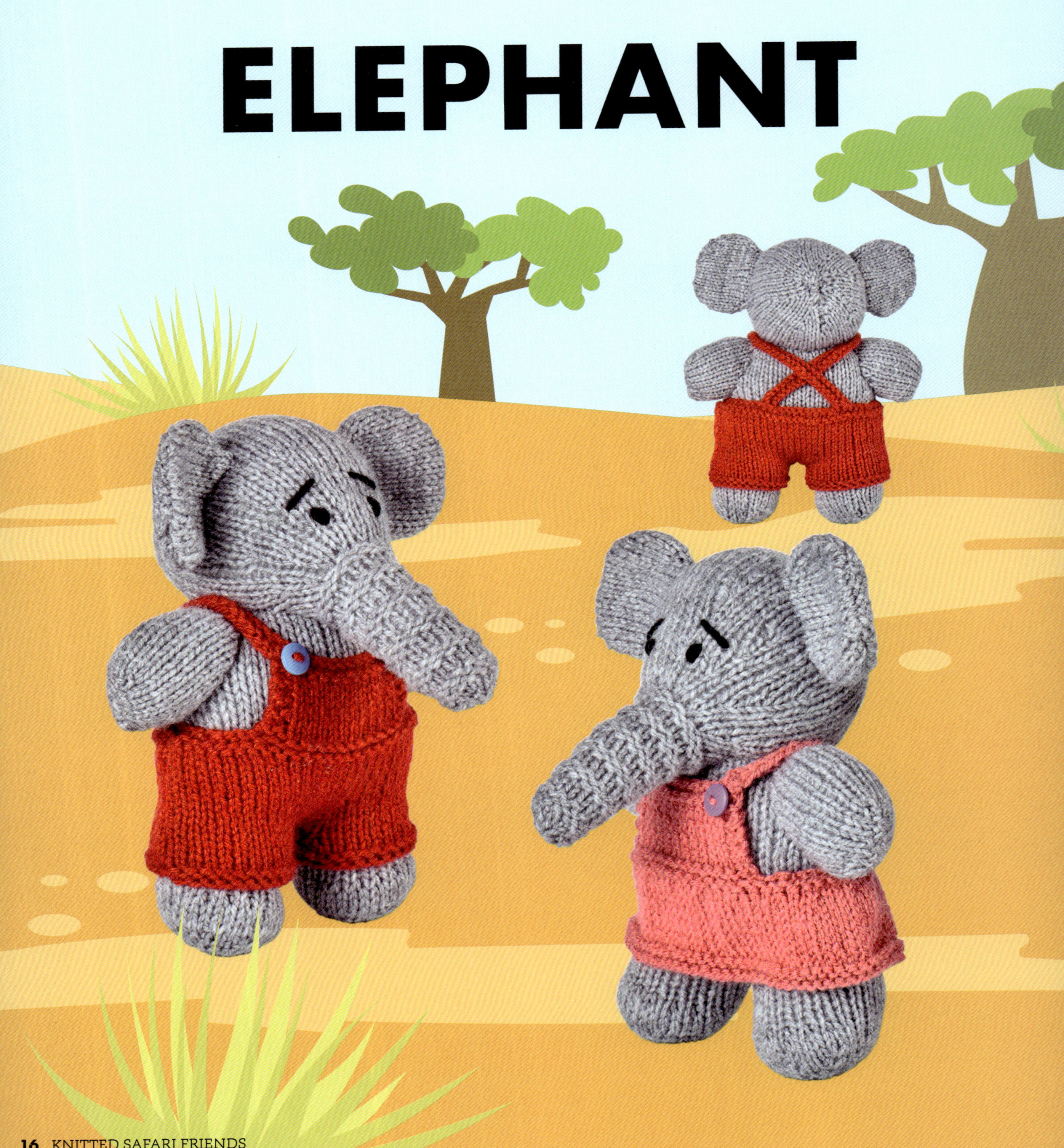

INFORMATION YOU'LL NEED

MATERIALS

Any DK (US: light worsted) yarn
(amounts given are approximate)
Yarn A grey (20g per Elephant)
Yarn B classic red (10g)
Yarn C rose pink (15g)
Oddment of black for embroidery
1 pair of 3.25mm (UK10:US3) needles and a spare needle of same size for dungarees
Knitters' pins and a blunt-ended needle for sewing up
Acrylic toy stuffing
2 small buttons for each Elephant

FINISHED SIZE

Elephant stands 7½in (19cm) tall

TENSION

26 sts x 34 rows measure 4in (10cm) square over st-st using 3.25mm needles and DK yarn before stuffing.

ABBREVIATIONS

See page 156

HOW TO MAKE ELEPHANT

BODY

Using the long tail method and yarn A, cast on 44 sts.

Row 1: Purl.

Row 2: K1, (k10, m1, k1, m1, k10) twice, k1 (48 sts).

Rows 3 to 11: Work 9 rows in st-st.

Rows 12 and 13: Work 2 rows in g-st to mark waist.

Rows 14 to 17: Beg with a k row, work 4 rows in st-st.

Row 18: K1, (k10, k3tog, k10) twice, k1 (44 sts).

Rows 19 to 21: Work 3 rows in st-st.

Row 22: K1, (k9, k3tog, k9) twice, k1 (40 sts).

Rows 23 to 25: Work 3 rows in st-st.

Row 26: K1, (k8, k3tog, k8) twice, k1 (36 sts).

Rows 27: Purl.

Cast off.

HEAD AND TRUNK

Using the long tail method and yarn A, cast on 8 sts.

Row 1 and foll 4 alt rows: Purl.

Row 2: (Kfb) to end (16 sts).

Row 4: (Kfb, k1) to end (24 sts).

Row 6: (Kfb, k2) to end (32 sts).

Row 8: (Kfb, k3) to end (40 sts).

Row 10: (Kfb, k4) to end (48 sts).

Rows 11 to 23: Work 13 rows in st-st.

Row 24: K4, (k2tog, k3) 4 times, (k3, k2tog) 4 times, k4 (40 sts).

Rows 25 to 27: Work 3 rows in st-st.

Row 28: K4, (k2tog, k2) 4 times, (k2, k2tog) 4 times, k4 (32 sts).

Rows 29 to 31: Work 3 rows in st-st.

Row 32: K4, (k2tog, k1) 4 times, (k1, k2tog) 4 times, k4 (24 sts).

Rows 33 to 35: Work 3 rows in st-st.

Row 36: K4, (k2tog) 8 times, k4 (16 sts).

Work trunk

Rows 37 and 38: K 1 row then p 1 row.

Rows 39 and 40: P 1 row then k 1 row.

Rows 41 to 44: Rep rows 37 to 40 once.

Row 45: K2tog, k to last 2 sts, k2tog (14 sts).

Row 46: Purl.

Rows 47 and 48: P 1 row then k 1 row.

Rows 49 and 50: K 1 row then p 1 row.

Rows 51 to 58: Rep rows 47 to 50 twice more.

Row 59: Purl.

Row 60: (K2tog) to end (7 sts).

Break yarn and thread through sts on needle, pull tight and secure by threading yarn a second time through sts.

LEGS (make 2)

Using the long tail method and yarn A, cast on 8 sts.

Row 1 and foll 2 alt rows: Purl.

Row 2: (Kfb) to end (16 sts).

Row 4: (Kfb, k1) to end (24 sts).

Row 6: (Kfb, k2) to end (32 sts).

Rows 7 to 9: Work 3 rows in st-st.

Row 10: K8, (k2tog) 8 times, k8 (24 sts).

Rows 11 to 19: Work 9 rows in st-st.

Cast off.

ARMS (make 2)

Using the long tail method and yarn A, cast on 16 sts.

Row 1: Purl.

Row 2: K1, (k1, m1, k5, m1, k1) twice, k1 (20 sts).

Rows 3 to 9: Beg with a p row, work 7 rows in st-st.

Rows 10 and 11: Cast off 2 sts at beg of next 2 rows (16 sts).

Row 12: K2tog, k to last 2 sts, k2tog (14 sts).

Row 13: Purl.

Rows 14 to 17: Rep rows 12 and 13 twice more (10 sts).

Row 18: (K2tog) to end (5 sts).

Cast off pwise.

DUNGAREES (make 2 pieces)

Note: Foll individual instructions as given for 1 front and 1 back of dungarees.

First leg

Using the long tail method and yarn B, cast on 16 sts and beg in g-st.

Rows 1 and 2: Work 2 rows in g-st.

Rows 3 and 4: K 1 row then p 1 row.

Break yarn and set aside.

Second leg

Work as for first leg but do not break yarn.

Join legs

Row 5: Beg with second leg and k14, k2tog, turn, using the knitting-on method cast on 5 sts, turn, then with the same yarn continue across first leg and k2tog, k to end (35 sts).

Rows 6 to 8: Work 3 rows in st-st.

Row 9: K15, k2tog, k1, k2tog, k15 (33 sts).

Row 10: Purl.

Row 11: K13, k2tog, k3, k2tog, k13, (31 sts).

Rows 12 to 18: Work 7 rows in st-st.

Rows 19 to 21: Work 3 rows in g-st ending with a RS row.

Cast off in g-st for back of dungarees or cont with bib for front of dungarees:

Divide for bib

Row 22: Cast off 8 sts kwise, k14 (15 sts now on RH needle), cast off rem 8 sts and fasten off.

Re-join yarn to rem sts and patt:

****Row 23:** K2, (k1 tbl) 11 times, k2 (15 sts).

Row 24: K2, p11, k2.
Row 25: Knit.
Rows 26 to 31: Rep rows 24 and 25, 3 times more, ending with a k row.
Rows 32 and 33: Work 2 rows in g-st, ending with a RS row.
Cast off in g-st.

STRAPS FOR DUNGAREES (make 2)

Using the long tail method and yarn B, cast on 30 sts.
Row 1: Knit.
Cast off kwise.

PINAFORE

Using the long tail method and yarn C, cast on 81 sts and beg in g-st.
Rows 1 and 2: Work 2 rows in g-st.
Rows 3 to 12: Beg with a k row, work 10 rows in st-st.
Row 13: K1, (k2tog, k2) to end (61 sts).
Rows 14 and 15: Work 2 rows in g-st ending with a RS row.
Divide for bib
Row 16: Cast off 23 sts kwise, k14 (15 sts now on RH needle) cast off rem 23 sts and fasten off.
Re-join yarn to rem sts and work bib from **, as for dungarees.

STRAPS FOR PINAFORE (make 2)

Make straps using yarn C, as for dungarees.

EARS (make 2)

Using the long tail method and yarn A, cast on 22 sts.
Row 1 and foll alt row: Purl.
Row 2: K1, (k1, m1, k8, m1 k1) twice, k1 (26 sts).
Row 4: K1, (k1, m1, k10, m1, k1) twice, k1 (30 sts).
Rows 5 to 9: Work 5 rows in st-st.
Row 10: K1, (k2tog, k10, k2tog tbl) twice, k1 (26 sts).
Row 11: Purl.
Row 12: K1, (k2tog, k8, k2tog tbl) twice, k1 (22 sts).
Row 13: P1, (p2tog tbl, p6, p2tog) twice, p1 (18 sts).
Cast off.

MAKING UP

Note: Sew up all row-end seams on right side using mattress stitch one stitch in from the edge, unless otherwise stated; a one-stitch seam allowance has been allowed for this.

BODY

Sew up side edges of body and with this seam at centre back, oversew cast-on stitches. Stuff body leaving neck open.

HEAD AND TRUNK

Sew up side edges of trunk and stuff trunk. Gather round cast-on stitches of head, pull tight and secure. Sew up side edges of head leaving a gap, stuff and sew up gap. Pin and sew head to body making a short horizontal stitch over one stitch from head then a short horizontal stitch over one stitch from body, and do this alternately all the way round.

LEGS

Gather round cast-on stitches of legs, pull tight and secure. Sew up side edges of legs and stuff. Pin legs to body leaving a ¾in (2cm) gap at crotch, and sew in place.

ARMS

Fold cast-on stitches of arms in half and oversew. Sew up side edges of arms from cast-on edge to cast-off stitches at under arm. Stuff, then pin and sew arms to sides of Elephant.

DUNGAREES, STRAPS AND BUTTONS

Place two pieces of dungarees together matching all edges and sew up inside leg seams and across crotch. Sew up side seams and place dungarees on Elephant. Sew cast-off stitches of waist of dungarees to row above waist of Elephant using back stitch all the way round. Sew ends of straps to top edge of front of bib, take straps over shoulders, cross over and sew to back of dungarees. Add two buttons to bib.

PINAFORE, STRAPS AND BUTTONS

Sew up side edges of skirt of pinafore and place pinafore on Elephant. Sew cast-off stitches of waist of pinafore to row above waist of Elephant using back stitch all the way round. Sew ends of straps to top edge of front of bib, take straps over shoulders, cross over and sew to back of pinafore. Add two buttons to bib.

EARS

Fold cast-off stitches of ears in half and oversew. Sew up side edges of ears then pin and sew ears to Elephant.

FEATURES

Mark position of eyes with two pins and embroider eyes in black making a vertical chain stitch for each eye then a second chain stitch on top of first. Embroider eyebrows in black using straight stitches (see page 155 for how to begin and fasten off invisibly for the embroidery).

HIPPO

INFORMATION YOU'LL NEED

MATERIALS

Any DK (US: light worsted) yarn (amounts given are approximate)
Yarn A denim blue (20g per Hippo)
Yarn B apple green (10g)
Yarn C yellow (15g)
Oddment of black for embroidery
1 pair of 3.25mm (UK10:US3) needles and a spare needle of same size for dungarees
Knitters' pins and a blunt-ended needle for sewing up
Tweezers (optional)
Acrylic toy stuffing
2 small buttons for each Hippo

FINISHED SIZE

Hippo stands 7½in (19cm) tall

TENSION

26 sts x 34 rows measure 4in (10cm) square over st-st using 3.25mm needles and DK yarn before stuffing.

ABBREVIATIONS

See page 156

HOW TO MAKE HIPPO

BODY

Make body using yarn A, as for Elephant on page 18.

HEAD

Using the long tail method and yarn A, cast on 36 sts.
Row 1: Purl.
Row 2: (K4, kfb, k4) 4 times (40 sts).
Rows 3 to 21: Work 19 rows in st-st.
Row 22: (K2tog, k3) to end (32 sts).
Row 23 and foll 2 alt rows: Purl.
Row 24: (K2tog, k2) to end (24 sts).
Row 26: (K2tog, k1) to end (16 sts).
Row 28: (K2tog) to end (8 sts).
Break yarn and thread through sts on needle, pull tight and secure by threading yarn a second time through sts.

MUZZLE

Using the long tail method and yarn A, cast on 32 sts.
Rows 1 to 3: Beg with a p row, work 3 rows in st-st.
Row 4: *K5, (m1, k2) 4 times, k3; rep from * once (40 sts).
Rows 5 to 13: Work 9 rows in st-st.
Row 14: *K6, (k2tog) 4 times, k6; rep from * once (32 sts).
Row 15 and foll alt row: Purl.
Row 16: *K4, (k2tog) 4 times, k4; rep from * once (24 sts).
Row 18: *K2, (k2tog) 4 times, k2; rep from * once (16 sts).
Row 19: Purl.
Cast off.

LEGS (make 2)

Using the long tail method and yarn A, cast on 8 sts.
Row 1 and foll 2 alt rows: Purl.
Row 2: (Kfb) to end (16 sts).
Row 4: (Kfb, k1) to end (24 sts).
Row 6: (Kfb, k2) to end (32 sts).
Rows 7 to 11: Work 5 rows in st-st.
Row 12: (K2tog, k2) to end (24 sts).
Rows 13 to 19: Work 7 rows in st-st.
Cast off.

ARMS (make 2)

Using the long tail method and yarn A, cast on 8 sts.
Row 1: Purl.
Row 2: (Kfb) to end (16 sts).
Rows 2 to 7: Work 5 rows in st-st.
Row 8: K6, (k2tog) twice, k6 (14 sts).
Row 9: Purl.
Row 10: K6, k2tog, k6 (13 sts).
Rows 11 to 23: Work 13 rows in st-st.
Row 24: K1, (k2tog, k1) to end (9 sts).
Break yarn and thread through sts on needle, and leave loose.

DUNGAREES
(make 2 pieces)

Note: Foll individual instructions as given for 1 front and 1 back of dungarees.

First leg

Using the long tail method and yarn B, cast on 16 sts and beg in g-st.

Rows 1 and 2: Work 2 rows in g-st.

Break yarn and set aside.

Second leg

Work as for first leg but do not break yarn.

Join legs

Row 3: Beg with second leg and k14, k2tog, turn, using the knitting-on method cast on 5 sts, turn, then with the same yarn continue across first leg and k2tog, k to end (35 sts).

Rows 4 to 6: Work 3 rows in st-st.

Row 7: K15, k2tog, k1, k2tog, k15 (33 sts).

Row 8: Purl.

Row 9: K13, k2tog, k3, k2tog, k13 (31 sts).

Rows 10 to 16: Work 7 rows in st-st.

Rows 17 to 19: Work 3 rows in g-st ending with a RS row.

Cast off in g-st for back of dungarees or cont with bib for front of dungarees:

Divide for bib

Row 20: Cast off 8 sts kwise, k14 (15 sts now on RH needle), cast off rem 8 sts and fasten off.

Re-join yarn to rem sts and patt:

****Row 21:** K2, (k1 tbl) 11 times, k2 (15 sts).

Row 22: K2, p11, k2.

Row 23: Knit.

Rows 24 to 29: Rep rows 22 and 23, 3 times more ending with a k row.

Rows 30 and 31: Work 2 rows in g-st, ending with a RS row.

Cast off in g-st.

STRAPS FOR DUNGAREES
(make 2)

Using the long tail method and yarn B, cast on 30 sts.

Row 1: Knit.

Cast off kwise.

PINAFORE

Using the long tail method and yarn C, cast on 81 sts and beg in g-st.

Rows 1 and 2: Work 2 rows in g-st.

Rows 3 to 12: Beg with a k row, work 10 rows in st-st.

Row 13: K1, (k2tog, k2) to end (61 sts).

Rows 14 and 15: Work 2 rows in g-st ending with a RS row.

Divide for bib

Row 16: Cast off 23 sts kwise, k14 (15 sts now on RH needle) cast off rem 23 sts and fasten off.

Re-join yarn to rem sts and work bib from **, as for dungarees.

STRAPS FOR PINAFORE
(make 2)

Make straps using yarn C, as for dungarees.

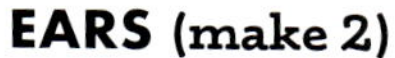

EARS (make 2)

Using the long tail method and yarn A, cast on 8 sts.
Row 1: Purl.
Row 2: (K1, m1) 3 times, k2, (m1, k1) 3 times (14 sts).
Rows 3 to 6: Work 4 rows in st-st, ending on a k row.
Row 7: P2, (p2tog, p2) to end (11 sts).
Break yarn and thread through sts on needle, pull tight and secure by threading yarn a second time through sts.

NOSTRILS (make 2)

Using the long tail method and yarn A, cast on 5 sts.
Rows 1 to 3: Beg with a p row, work 3 rows in st-st.
Cast off.

MAKING UP

Note: Sew up all row-end seams on right side using mattress stitch one stitch in from the edge, unless otherwise stated; a one-stitch seam allowance has been allowed for this.

BODY

Sew up side edges of body and with this seam at centre back, oversew cast-on stitches. Stuff body leaving neck open.

HEAD AND MUZZLE

Sew up side edges of head and stuff head leaving neck open. Pin and sew head to body making a short horizontal stitch over one stitch from head then a short horizontal stitch over one stitch from body, and do this alternately all the way round. Sew up side edges of muzzle and with seam at centre of underneath, sew across cast-off stitches. Stuff muzzle then pin and sew muzzle to Hippo.

LEGS

Gather round cast-on stitches of legs, pull tight and secure. Sew up side edges of legs and stuff. Pin legs to body, leaving a ¾in (2cm) gap at crotch, and sew in place.

ARMS

Fold cast-on stitches of arms in half and oversew. Sew up side edges of hands and stuff hands. Sew up side edges of arms and stuff arms with tweezers or tip of scissors. Pull stitches on a thread tight and secure. Sew arms to body at each side.

DUNGAREES, STRAPS AND BUTTONS

Make up dungarees, straps and buttons, as for Elephant on page 22.

PINAFORE, STRAPS AND BUTTONS

Make up pinafore, straps and buttons, as for Elephant on page 22.

EARS

Sew up side edges of ears and with this seam at centre back, pin and sew ears to Hippo.

FEATURES

Mark position of eyes with two pins above muzzle and embroider eyes in black, making a vertical chain stitch for each eye then a second chain stitch on top of first. Embroider eyebrows in black using straight stitches (see page 155 for how to begin and fasten off invisibly for the embroidery).

NOSTRILS

Fold nostrils and oversew cast-on and cast-off stitches. Using picture as a guide, curl nostrils and pin and sew nostrils to muzzle.

LION

INFORMATION YOU'LL NEED

MATERIALS

Any DK (US: light worsted) yarn
(amounts given are approximate)
Yarn A yellow (20g)
Yarn B white (5g)
Yarn C black (5g)
Yarn D terracotta (15g)
Yarn E purple (10g)
Oddment of black for embroidery
1 pair of 3.25mm (UK10:US3) needles and a spare needle of same size for dungarees
Knitters' pins and a blunt-ended needle for sewing up
Acrylic toy stuffing
2 small buttons

FINISHED SIZE

Lion stands 8in (20.5cm) tall

TENSION

26 sts x 34 rows measure 4in (10cm) square over st-st using 3.25mm needles and DK yarn before stuffing.

ABBREVIATIONS

See page 156

SPECIAL ABBREVIATION

w1: wrap 1 stitch – take yarn between needles to opposite side, slip 1 stitch pwise from LH needle to RH needle, then take yarn between needles to first side.

HOW TO MAKE LION

BODY

Using the long tail method and yarn A, cast on 40 sts.

Row 1: Purl.

Row 2: K1, (k9, m1, k1, m1, k9) twice, k1 (44 sts).

Rows 3 to 9: Beg with a p row, work 7 rows in st-st.

Rows 10 and 11: Work 2 rows in g-st to mark waist.

Rows 12 to 21: Beg with a k row, work 10 rows in st-st.

Row 22: K1, (k9, k3tog, k9) twice, k1 (40 sts).

Row 23: Purl.

Row 24: K1, (k8, k3tog, k8) twice, k1 (36 sts).

Row 25: Purl.

Cast off.

HEAD

Using the long tail method and yarn A, cast on 36 sts.

Row 1: Purl.

Row 2: (K8, m1, k2, m1, k8) twice (40 sts).

Rows 3 to 17: Work 15 rows in st-st.

Row 18: (K2tog, k3) to end (32 sts).

Row 19 and foll 2 alt rows: Purl.

Row 20: (K2tog, k2) to end (24 sts).

Row 22: (K2tog, k1) to end (16 sts).

Row 24: (K2tog) to end (8 sts).

Break yarn and thread through sts on needle, pull tight and secure by threading yarn a second time through sts.

MUZZLE

First piece

Using the long tail method and yarn A, cast on 12 sts.

Row 1 and foll 3 alt rows: Purl.

Row 2: K2tog, k8, k2tog (10 sts).

Row 4: K2tog, k6, k2tog (8 sts).

Row 6: K2tog, k4, k2tog (6 sts).

Row 8: K2tog, k2, k2tog (4 sts).

Break yarn and thread through sts on needle, pull tight and secure by threading yarn a second time through sts.

Second piece

Using the long tail method and yarn B, cast on 23 sts.

Row 1 and foll 3 alt rows: Purl.

Row 2: K2tog, k to last 2 sts, k2tog (21 sts).

Row 4: K2tog, k7, k3tog, k7, k2tog (17 sts).

Row 6: K2tog, k5, k3tog, k5, k2tog (13 sts).

Row 8: K2tog, k3, k3tog, k3, k2tog (9 sts).

Break yarn and thread through sts on needle, pull tight and secure by threading yarn a second time through sts.

NOSE

Using the long tail method and yarn C, cast on 5 sts.

Rows 1 and 2: P 1 row then k 1 row.

Row 3: P1, p3tog, p1 (3 sts).

Break yarn and thread through sts on needle, pull tight and secure by threading yarn a second time through sts.

MANE

Using the long tail method and yarn D, cast on 30 sts loosely.

Row 1: K1, *k next st placing index finger of LH behind RH needle and wind yarn round finger and needle clockwise twice, then wind just round needle in the same direction once, knit st pulling 3 loops through, place these loops on LH needle and k into the back of them, pull on loops just made to secure (this will be referred to as loop-st), rep from * to last st, k1.

Row 2: K24 sts, w1 (see special abbreviation), turn.

Row 3: S1p, (loop-st) 18 times, w1, turn.

Row 4: S1p, k to end.

Row 5: K1, (loop-st) to last st, k1.

Row 6: K22, w1, turn.

Row 7: S1p, (loop-st) 14 times, w1, turn.

Row 8: S1p, (k2, k2tog) 3 times, k to end (27 sts).

Row 9: K1, (loop-st) to last st, k1.

Row 10: K21, w1, turn.

Row 11: S1p, (loop-st) 15 times, w1, turn.

Row 12: S1p, k2tog, k3, k2tog, k1, k2tog, k3, k2tog, k to end (23 sts).

Row 13: K1, (loop-st) to last st, k1.
Row 14: K8, k2tog, k3, k2tog, k8 (21 sts).
Row 15: As row 13.
Row 16: K5, (k2tog, k1) 4 times, k4 (17 sts).
Row 17: As row 13.
Row 18: K6, k2tog, k1, k2tog, k6 (15 sts).
Row 19: As row 13.
Row 20: (K1, k2tog) twice, k3, (k2tog, k1) twice (11 sts).
Row 21: As row 13.
Row 22: K2tog, (k1, k2tog) to end (7 sts).
Row 23: K1, (loop-st) to last st, k1.
Cast off kwise.

FEET AND LEGS (make 2)

Using the long tail method and yarn A, cast on 16 sts.
Row 1: Purl.
Row 2: (K1, kfb) 4 times, (kfb, k1) 4 times (24 sts).
Rows 3 to 9: Work 7 rows in st-st.
Row 10: K6, (k2tog) 6 times, k6 (18 sts).
Row 11: Purl.
Row 12: K7, (k2tog) twice, k7 (16 sts).
Rows 13 to 21: Work 9 rows in st-st.
Cast off.

HANDS AND FOREARMS (make 2)

Using the long tail method and yarn A, cast on 8 sts.
Row 1 and foll alt row: Purl.
Row 2: (Kfb) to end (16 sts).
Row 4: (Kfb, k3) to end (20 sts).
Rows 5 to 9: Work 5 rows in st-st.
Row 10: K2tog, (k1, k2tog) to end (13 sts).
Rows 11 to 21: Work 11 rows in st-st.
Row 22: K1, (k2tog, k1) to end (9 sts).
Break yarn, thread through sts on needle and leave loose.

DUNGAREES (make 2 pieces)

Note: Foll individual instructions as given for 1 front and 1 back of dungarees.

First leg
Using the long tail method and yarn E, cast on 12 sts and beg in g-st.
Rows 1 and 2: Work 2 rows in g-st.
Break yarn and set aside.

Second leg
Work as for first leg but do not break yarn.

Join legs
Row 3: Beg with second leg and k10, k2tog, turn, using the knitting-on method cast on 5 sts, turn, then with the same yarn continue across first leg and k2tog, k to end (27 sts).
Row 4 and foll 2 alt rows: Purl.
Row 5: K2, m1, k23, m1, k2 (29 sts).
Row 7: K12, k2tog, k1, k2tog, k12 (27 sts).
Row 9: K10, k2tog, k3, k2tog, k10 (25 sts).
Rows 10 to 14: Work 5 rows in st-st.
Rows 15 to 17: Work 3 rows in g-st, ending with a RS row.
Cast off in g-st for back of dungarees or cont with bib for front of dungarees:

Divide for bib
Row 18: Cast off 6 sts kwise, k12 (13 sts now on RH needle), cast off rem 6 sts and fasten off.
Rejoin yarn to rem sts and patt:
Row 19: K2, (k1 tbl) 9 times, k2 (13 sts).
Row 20: K2, p9, k2.
Row 21: Knit.
Rows 22 to 27: Rep rows 20 and 21, 3 times more, ending with a k row.
Rows 28 and 29: Work 2 rows in g-st, ending with a RS row.
Cast off in g-st.

STRAPS FOR DUNGAREES (make 2)

Using the long tail method and yarn E, cast on 28 sts.
Row 1: Knit.
Cast off kwise.

EARS (make 2)

Using the long tail method and yarn A, cast on 8 sts.

Row 1: Purl.

Row 2: (K1, m1) 3 times, k2, (m1, k1) 3 times (14 sts).

Rows 3 to 6: Work 4 rows in st-st, ending on a k row.

Row 7: P2, (p2tog, p2) to end (11 sts).

Break yarn and thread through sts on needle, pull tight and secure by threading yarn a second time through sts.

TAIL

Using the long tail method and yarn A, cast on 10 sts.

Rows 1 to 5: Beg with a p row, work 5 rows in st-st.

Cast off.

Tip of tail

Using the long tail method and yarn D, cast on 8 sts and work in g-st.

Rows 1 to 5: Work 5 rows in g-st.

Cast off in g-st.

MAKING UP

Note: Sew up all row-end seams on right side using mattress stitch one stitch in from the edge, unless otherwise stated; a one-stitch seam allowance has been allowed for this.

BODY

Sew up side edges of body and with this seam at centre back, oversew cast-on stitches. Stuff body leaving neck open.

HEAD

Sew up side edges of head and stuff leaving neck open. Pin and sew head to body, making a horizontal stitch over one stitch from head then a horizontal stitch over one stitch from body, and do this alternately all the way round.

MUZZLE AND NOSE

Place stitches pulled tight on a thread of first and second piece of muzzle together and sew up side edges. Stuff then pin and sew muzzle to head. Sew on nose.

MANE

Sew up side edges of mane and place on head. Sew around outside edge of mane.

FEET AND LEGS

Fold cast-on stitches of feet in half and oversew. Sew up side edges of legs and stuff feet and legs. Pin legs to body, leaving a ¾in (2cm) gap at crotch, and sew in place.

HANDS AND FOREARMS

Gather round cast-on stitches of hands, pull tight and secure. Sew up side edges of forearms and stuff. Pull stitches on a thread tight and secure. Sew forearms to Lion at both sides.

DUNGAREES, STRAPS AND BUTTONS

Make up dungarees, straps and buttons, as for Elephant on page 22.

EARS

Sew up side edges of ears and press flat. Position ears and sew to head.

FEATURES

Mark position of eyes with two pins and embroider eyes in black, making a vertical chain stitch for each eye then a second chain stitch on top of first. Sew on nose and embroider eyebrows and mouth in black using straight stitches. Embroider three claws on each hand and foot using straight stitches (see page 155 for how to begin and fasten off invisibly for the embroidery).

TAIL

Fold tail and oversew cast-on and cast-off stitches. Fold tip of tail and sew to end of tail. Sew tail to Lion at back.

ZEBRA

INFORMATION YOU'LL NEED

MATERIALS

Any DK (US: light worsted) yarn (amounts given are approximate)
Yarn A white (20g)
Yarn B black (20g)
Yarn C zest (5g)
Yarn D petrol blue (5g)
Oddment of grey for embroidery
1 pair of 3.25mm (UK10:US3) needles and a spare needle of the same size
Knitters' pins and a blunt-ended needle for sewing up
Tweezers (optional)
Acrylic toy stuffing
2 small buttons

FINISHED SIZE

Zebra stands 7½in (19cm) tall

TENSION

26 sts x 34 rows measure 4in (10cm) square over st-st using 3.25mm needles and DK yarn before stuffing.

ABBREVIATIONS

See page 156

HOW TO MAKE ZEBRA

BODY

Using the long tail method and yarn A, cast on 32 sts.

Row 1: Purl.

Row 2: K1, (k7, m1, k1, m1, k7) twice, k1 (36 sts).

Rows 3 to 9: Work 7 rows in st-st.

Rows 10 and 11: Work 2 rows in g-st to mark waist.

Rows 12 and 13: K 1 row then p 1 row.

Join on yarn B and work in stripes carrying yarn loosely up side of work:

Rows 14 and 15: Yarn B-k 1 row then p 1 row.

Rows 16 and 17: Yarn A-k 1 row then p 1 row.

Rows 18 to 21: Rep rows 14 to 17 once.

Row 22: Yarn B-k1, (k7, k3tog, k7) twice, k1 (32 sts).

Row 23: Purl.

Row 24: Yarn A-k1, (k6, k3tog, k6) twice, k1 (28 sts).

Row 25: Purl.

Row 26: Yarn B-k1, (k5, k3tog, k5) twice, k1 (24 sts).

Row 27: Purl.

Cast off in yarn B.

HEAD

Using the long tail method and yarn B, cast on 16 sts loosely.

Row 1: (Pfb, k1) to end (24 sts).

Join on yarn A and work in stripes carrying yarn loosely up side of work:

Row 2: Yarn A-knit.

Row 3: (Pfb, p3) to end (30 sts).

Row 4: Yarn B-knit.

Row 5: (Pfb, p4) to end (36 sts).

Rows 6 and 7: Yarn A-k 1 row then p 1 row.

Rows 8 and 9: Yarn B-k 1 row then p 1 row.

Rows 10 to 17: Rep rows 6 to 9 twice more.

Row 18: Yarn A-k6, (k2tog, k2) twice, k10, (k2tog, k2) twice, k4 (32 sts).

Row 19: Purl.

Row 20: Yarn B-k4, (k2tog) 4 times, k8, (k2tog) 4 times, k4 (24 sts).

Row 21: Purl.

Rows 22 and 23: Yarn A-k 1 row then p 1 row.

Row 24: Yarn B-k2, (k2tog) 4 times, k4, (k2tog) 4 times, k2 (16 sts).

Rows 25 to 29: Work 5 rows in st-st.

Cont in yarn A and shape:

Row 30: Yarn A-k3, k2tog, k6, k2tog, k3 (14 sts).

Rows 31 to 33: Work 3 rows in st-st.

Cast off.

LEGS (make 2)

Using the long tail method and yarn A, cast on 8 sts.

Row 1: (Kfb) to end (16 sts).

Row 2: K 1 row for fold line.

Rows 3 and 4: K 1 row then p 1 row.

Join on yarn B and work in stripes, carrying yarn loosely up side of work:

Rows 5 and 6: Yarn B-k 1 row then p 1 row.

Rows 7 and 8: Yarn A-k 1 row, then p 1 row.

Rows 9 to 16: Rep rows 5 to 8 twice more.

Cast off in yarn A.

HOOVES FOR LEGS

(make 2)

Using the long tail method and yarn B, cast on 8 sts.

Row 1: (Kfb) to end (16 sts).
Row 2: Purl.
Row 3: (Kfb, k1) to end (24 sts).
Row 4: K 1 row for fold line.
Rows 5 and 6: K 1 row then p 1 row.
Row 7: (K2tog, k1) to end (16 sts).
Row 8: Purl.
Cast off.

FOREARMS (make 2)

Using the long tail method and yarn A, cast on 6 sts.

Row 1: (Kfb) to end (12 sts).
Row 2: K 1 row for fold line.
Rows 3 and 4: K 1 row then p 1 row.
Join on yarn B and work in stripes, carrying yarn loosely up side of work:
Rows 5 and 6: Yarn B, k 1 row then p 1 row.
Rows 7 and 8: Yarn A, k 1 row then p 1 row.
Rows 9 to 16: Rep rows 5 to 8 twice more.
Row 17: Yarn B-knit.
Row 18: (P2tog) to end (6 sts).
Break yarn, thread through sts on needle and leave loose.

HOOVES FOR FOREARMS

(make 2)

Using the long tail method and yarn B, cast on 6 sts.

Row 1: (Kfb) to end (12 sts).
Row 2: Purl.
Row 3: (Kfb, k1) to end (18 sts).
Row 4: K 1 row for fold line.
Rows 5 and 6: K 1 row, then p 1 row.
Row 7: (K2tog, k1) to end (12 sts).
Row 8: Purl.
Cast off.

TROUSERS (make 2 pieces)

First leg

Using the long tail method and yarn C, cast on 12 sts and beg in g-st.

Rows 1 and 2: Work 2 rows in g-st.

Break yarn and set aside.

Second leg

Work as for first leg but do not break yarn.

Join legs

Row 3: Beg with second leg and k10, k2tog, turn, using the knitting-on method cast on 5 sts, turn, then with the same yarn continue across first leg and k2tog, k to end (27 sts).

Rows 4 to 6: Beg with a p row, work 3 rows in st-st.

Row 7: K11, k2tog, k1, k2tog, k11 (25 sts).

Row 8: Purl.

Row 9: K9, k2tog, k3, k2tog, k9, (23 sts).

Rows 10 to 14: Work 5 rows in st-st.

Rows 15 to 17: Work 3 rows in g-st, ending with a RS row.

Cast off in g-st.

BRACES (make 2)

Using the long tail method and yarn D, cast on 30 sts.

Row 1: Knit.

Cast off kwise.

EARS (make 2)

Using the long tail method and yarn B, cast on 10 sts.

Rows 1 to 3: Beg with a p row, work 3 rows in st-st.

Row 4: (K2tog) to end (5 sts).

Row 5: Purl.

Break yarn and thread through sts on needle, pull tight and secure by threading yarn a second time through sts.

MANE

Using the long tail method and yarn B, cast on 30 sts loosely, work in loop-st and at the same time cast off, as foll:

Row 1: K1, *place index finger of LH behind RH needle and wind yarn round finger and needle clockwise twice, then wind just round needle in the same direction once. Knit st pulling 3 loops through, place these loops on LH needle and k into the back of them, pass first st on RH needle over second st and off the needle. Pull on loops just made to secure (this will be referred to as loop-st), rep from * to last st, k1 (2 sts).

Row 2: Pass second st over first and off the needle (1 st).

Fasten off.

MAKING UP

Note: Sew up all row-end seams on right side using mattress stitch one stitch in from the edge, unless otherwise stated; a one-stitch seam allowance has been allowed for this.

BODY

Sew up side edges of body and with this seam at centre back, oversew cast-on stitches. Stuff body leaving neck open.

HEAD

Gather round cast-on stitches of head, pull tight and secure. Sew up side edges leaving a gap. With seam at centre of underneath, sew across cast-off stitches. Stuff head and sew up gap. Pin and sew head to body with nose pointing down.

LEGS AND HOOVES

Gather round cast-on stitches of legs, pull tight and secure. Sew up side edges of legs and stuff legs. Pin legs to body, leaving a ¾in (2cm) gap at crotch, and sew in place. Gather round cast-on stitches of hooves, pull tight and secure. Sew up side edges of hooves and stuff with tweezers or tip of scissors. Sew hooves to ends of legs taking a horizontal stitch over one stitch from hoof then a horizontal stitch over one stitch from leg, and do this alternately all the way round.

ARMS AND HOOVES

Gather round cast-on stitches of arms, pull tight and secure. Sew up side edges of arms and stuff. Pull stitches on a thread tight and secure. Make up hooves and sew hooves to ends of arms, as for legs. Sew arms to Zebra.

TROUSERS, BRACES AND BUTTONS

Place two pieces of trousers together matching all edges and sew up inside leg seams and across crotch. Sew up side seams and place trousers on Zebra. Sew waist of trousers to waist of Zebra using back stitch all the way round. Place braces over top edge of waist of front of trousers at each side and sew in place. Take braces over shoulders, cross over, and sew ends to waist of trousers at back. Add two buttons to front of trousers.

EARS

Oversew side edges of ears and press flat. Sew ears to head.

MANE

Fold mane in half and oversew together. Pin and sew mane to head.

FEATURES

Mark position of eyes with two pins and embroider eyes in grey making a vertical chain stitch for each eye then a second chain stitch on top of first. Embroider nostrils in grey using straight stitches (see page 155 for how to begin and fasten off invisibly for the embroidery).

TIGER

INFORMATION YOU'LL NEED

MATERIALS

Any DK (US: light worsted) yarn
(amounts given are approximate)
Yarn A orange (20g)
Yarn B dark brown (5g)
Yarn C white (5g)
Yarn D black (5g)
Yarn E blue (10g)
Yarn F grey (5g)
Oddments of black and dark brown for embroidery
1 pair of 3.25mm (UK10:US3) needles and a spare needle of same size for dungarees
Knitters' pins and a blunt-ended needle for sewing up
Acrylic toy stuffing
2 small buttons

FINISHED SIZE

Tiger stands 7½in (19cm) tall

TENSION

26 sts x 34 rows measure 4in (10cm) square over st-st using 3.25mm needles and DK yarn before stuffing.

ABBREVIATIONS

See page 156

HOW TO MAKE TIGER

BODY

Using the long tail method and yarn A, cast on 36 sts.

Row 1: Purl.

Row 2: K1, (k8, m1, k1, m1, k8) twice, k1 (40 sts).

Rows 3 to 9: Beg with a p row, work 7 rows in st-st.

Rows 10 and 11: Work 2 rows in g-st to mark waist.

Rows 12 and 13: K 1 row then p 1 row.

Join on yarn B and work in stripes, carrying yarn loosely up side of work:

Rows 14 and 15: Yarn B-work 2 rows in st-st.

Rows 16 to 19: Yarn A-work 4 rows in st-st.

Row 20: Yarn B-k1, (k8, k3tog, k8) twice, k1 (36 sts).

Row 21: Purl.

Row 22: Yarn A-k1, (k7, k3tog, k7) twice, k1 (32 sts).

Row 23: Purl.

Row 24: K1, (k6, k3tog, k6) twice, k1 (28 sts).

Row 25: Purl.

Cast off.

HEAD

Using the long tail method and yarn A, cast on 28 sts.

Row 1: Purl.

Row 2: K3, (m1, k2) to last st, k1 (40 sts).

Row 3: Purl.

Join on yarn B and work in stripes, carrying yarn loosely up side of work.

Rows 4 and 5: Yarn B-work 2 rows in st-st.

Rows 6 to 9: Yarn A-work 4 rows in st-st.

Rows 10 and 11: Yarn B-work 2 rows in st-st.

Rows 12 to 19: Yarn A-work 8 rows in st-st.

Row 20: (K2tog, k3) to end (32 sts).

Row 21 and foll 2 alt row: Purl.

Row 22: (K2tog, k2) to end (24 sts).

Row 24: (K2tog, k1) to end (16 sts).

Row 26: (K2tog) to end (8 sts).

Break yarn and thread through sts on needle, pull tight and secure by threading yarn a second time through sts.

MUZZLE

First piece

Using the long tail method and yarn A, cast on 10 sts.

Row 1 and foll 2 alt rows: Purl.

Row 2: K2tog, k6, k2tog (8 sts).

Row 4: K2tog, k4, k2tog (6 sts).

Row 6: K2tog, k2, k2tog (4 sts).

Break yarn and thread through sts on needle, pull tight and secure by threading yarn a second time through sts.

Second piece

Using the long tail method and yarn C, cast on 21 sts.

Row 1 and foll 2 alt rows: Purl.

Row 2: K2tog, k7, k3tog, k7, k2tog (17 sts).

Row 4: K2tog, k5, k3tog, k5, k2tog (13 sts).

Row 6: K2tog, k3, k3tog, k3, k2tog (9 sts).

Break yarn and thread through sts on needle, pull tight and secure by threading yarn a second time through sts.

NOSE

Using the long tail method and yarn D, cast on 5 sts.

Rows 1 and 2: P 1 row then k 1 row.

Row 3: P1, p3tog, p1 (3 sts).

Break yarn and thread through sts on needle, pull tight and secure by threading yarn a second time through sts.

FEET AND LEGS (make 2)

Using the long tail method and yarn C, cast on 16 sts.

Row 1: Purl.

Row 2: (K1, kfb) 4 times, (kfb, k1) 4 times (24 sts).

Rows 3 to 9: Work 7 rows in st-st.

Change to yarn A and dec:

Row 10: K4, (k2tog) 8 times, k4 (16 sts).

Row 11: Purl.

Join on yarn B and work in stripes, carrying yarn loosely up side of work.

Rows 12 and 13: Yarn B-work 2 rows in st-st.

Rows 14 to 17: Yarn A-work 4 rows in st-st.

Rows 18 and 19: Yarn B-work 2 rows in st-st.

Rows 20 and 21: Yarn A-work 2 rows in st-st.

Cast off in yarn A.

HANDS AND FOREARMS (make 2)

Using the long tail method and yarn C, cast on 8 sts.

Row 1 and foll alt row: Purl.

Row 2: (Kfb) to end (16 sts).

Row 4: (Kfb, k3) to end (20 sts).

Rows 5 to 9: Work 5 rows in st-st.

Change to yarn A and dec:

Row 10: K2tog, (k1, k2tog) to end (13 sts).

Row 11: Purl.

Join on yarn B and work in stripes, carrying yarn loosely up side of work.

Rows 12 and 13: Yarn B-k 1 row then p 1 row.

Rows 14 to 17: Yarn A-work 4 rows in st-st.

Rows 18 and 19: Yarn B-work 2 rows in st-st.

Cont in yarn A:

Rows 20 to 23: Work 4 rows in st-st.

Row 24: K1, (k2tog, k1) to end (9 sts).

Break yarn, thread through sts on needle and leave loose.

TROUSERS (make 2 pieces)

First leg

Using the long tail method and yarn E, cast on 12 sts and beg in g-st.

Rows 1 and 2: Work 2 rows in g-st.

Break yarn and set aside.

Second leg

Work as for first leg but do not break yarn.

Join legs

Row 3: Beg with second leg and k10, k2tog, turn, using the knitting-on method cast on 5 sts, turn, then with the same yarn continue across first leg and k2tog, k to end (27 sts).

Row 4 and foll 2 alt rows: Purl.

Row 5: K2, m1, k23, m1, k2 (29 sts).

Row 7: K12, k2tog, k1, k2tog, k12 (27 sts).

Row 9: K10, k2tog, k3, k2tog, k10 (25 sts).

Rows 10 to 14: Work 5 rows in st-st.

Rows 15 to 17: Work 3 rows in g-st, ending with a RS row.

Cast off in g-st.

BRACES (make 2)

Using the long tail method and yarn F, cast on 28 sts.

Row 1: Knit.

Cast off kwise.

EARS (make 2)

Using the long tail method and yarn A, cast on 16 sts.

Rows 1 to 5: Work 5 rows in st-st.

Row 6: K1, (k2tog, k1) to end (11 sts).

Break yarn and thread through sts on needle, pull tight and secure by threading yarn a second time through sts.

TAIL

Using the long tail method and yarn A, cast on 20 sts.

Rows 1 to 5: Beg with a p row, work 5 rows in st-st.

Row 6: Yarn B-k2tog, k to end (19 sts).

Row 7: Purl.

Rows 8 to 11: Yarn A-work 4 rows in st-st.

Rows 12 to 35: Rep rows 6 to 11, 4 times more (15 sts).

Row 36: (K2tog, k1) to end (10 sts).

Break yarn and thread through sts on needle, pull tight and secure by threading yarn a second time through sts.

MAKING UP

Note: Sew up all row-end seams on right side using mattress stitch one stitch in from the edge, unless otherwise stated; a one-stitch seam allowance has been allowed for this.

BODY

Sew up side edges of body and, with this seam at centre back, oversew cast-on stitches. Stuff body leaving neck open.

HEAD

Sew up side edges of head and stuff leaving neck open. Pin and sew head to body by making a horizontal stitch over one stitch from head then a horizontal stitch over one stitch from body, and do this alternately all the way round.

MUZZLE AND NOSE

Place stitches pulled tight together of first and second piece of muzzle and sew up side edges. Stuff then pin and sew muzzle to head. Sew on nose.

FEET AND LEGS

Fold cast-on stitches of feet in half and oversew. Sew up side edges of legs and stuff feet and legs. Pin legs to body, leaving a ¾in (2cm) gap at crotch, and sew in place.

HANDS AND FOREARMS

Gather round cast-on stitches of forearms, pull tight and secure. Sew up side edges of forearms and stuff. Pull stitches on a thread tight and secure. Sew forearms to Tiger at both sides.

TROUSERS, STRAPS AND BUTTONS

Make up trousers, straps and buttons, as for Zebra on page 43.

EARS

Sew up side edges of ears and with seam at centre back, press flat. Position ears and pin and sew ears to head.

FEATURES

Mark position of eyes with two pins and embroider eyes in black making a vertical chain stitch for each eye then a second chain stitch on top of first. Sew on nose and embroider eyebrows and mouth in black using straight stitches. Embroider 3 stripes in dark brown at top of head making straight double stitches (see page 155 for how to begin and fasten off invisibly for the embroidery).

TAIL

Roll tail up from decreasing row ends to long edge and sew long edge down. Gather round cast-on stitches, pull tight and secure. Sew tail to back below waistband sewing through trousers to body.

GIRAFFE

INFORMATION YOU'LL NEED

MATERIALS

Any DK (US: light worsted) yarn
(amounts given are approximate)
Yarn A yellow (20g)
Yarn B mustard (5g)
Yarn C cream (5g)
Yarn D brown (5g)
Yarn E orange (10g)
Yarn F grey (5g)
Oddment of black for embroidery
1 pair of 3.25mm (UK10:US3) needles and a spare needle of the same size
Knitters' pins and a blunt-ended needle for sewing up
Tweezers (optional)
Acrylic toy stuffing
2 small buttons

FINISHED SIZE

Giraffe stands 10in (25.5cm) tall

TENSION

26 sts x 34 rows measure 4in (10cm) square over st-st using 3.25mm needles and DK yarn before stuffing.

ABBREVIATIONS

See page 156

HOW TO MAKE GIRAFFE

BODY

Using the long tail method and yarn A, cast on 28 sts.

Row 1: Purl.

Row 2: K1, (k6, m1, k1, m1, k6) twice, k1 (32 sts).

Rows 3 to 9: Work 7 rows in st-st.

Rows 10 and 11: Work 2 rows in g-st to mark waist.

Rows 12 and 13: K 1 row then p 1 row.

Join on yarn B and work in stripes, 2 rows yarn B then 2 rows yarn A, and do this alternately, carrying yarn loosely up side of work, as foll:

Rows 14 and 15: Yarn B-k 1 row then p 1 row.

Rows 16 and 17: Yarn A-k1 row then p 1 row.

Rows 18 to 31: Rep rows 14 to 17, 3 times more then rows 14 and 15 once.

Row 32: Yarn A-k1, (k6, k3tog, k6) twice, k1 (28 sts).

Row 33: Purl.

Row 34: Yarn B-k1, (k5, k3tog, k5) twice, k1 (24 sts).

Row 35: Purl.

Row 36: Yarn A-k1, (k4, k3tog, k4) twice, k1 (20 sts).

Row 37: Purl.

Rows 38 and 39: Yarn B-k 1 row then p 1 row.

Row 40: Yarn A-k1, (k3, k3tog, k3) twice, k1 (16 sts).

Row 41: Purl.

Rows 42 and 43: Yarn B-k 1 row then p 1 row.

Cast off.

HEAD

Using the long tail method and yarn A, cast on 8 sts.

Row 1 and foll 2 alt rows: Purl.

Row 2: (Kfb) to end (16 sts).

Row 4: (Kfb, k1) to end (24 sts).

Row 6: (Kfb, k2) to end (32 sts).

Rows 7 to 15: Work 9 rows in st-st.

Row 16: (K2tog, k2) to end (24 sts).

Rows 17 and 19: Work 3 rows in st-st.

Change to yarn C and dec:

Row 20: (K2tog, k2) to end (18 sts).

Rows 21 to 23: Work 3 rows in st-st.

Row 24: K2, (k2tog, k2) to end (14 sts).

Rows 25 to 27: Work 3 rows in st-st.

Cast off.

HOOVES AND LEGS (make 2)

Using the long tail method and yarn D, cast on 7 sts.

Row 1: (Kfb) to end (14 sts).

Row 2: Purl.

Row 3: (Kfb, k1) to end (21 sts).

Row 4: K 1 row for fold line.

Rows 5 to 7: Beg with a k row, work 3 rows in st-st, ending on a k row.

Change to yarn A and dec:

Row 8: (P2tog, p1) to end (14 sts).

Rows 9 to 28: Work 20 rows in st-st.

Cast off.

TROUSERS (make 2 pieces)

First leg

Using the long tail method and yarn E, cast on 12 sts and beg in g-st.

Rows 1 and 2: Work 2 rows in g-st.

Rows 3 and 4: K 1 row then p 1 row.

Break yarn and set aside.

Second leg

Work as for first leg but do not break yarn.

Join legs

Row 5: Beg with second leg and k10, k2tog, turn, using the knitting-on method cast on 5 sts, turn, then with the same yarn continue across first leg and k2tog, k to end (27 sts).

Rows 6 to 8: Beg with a p row, work 3 rows in st-st.

Row 9: K11, k2tog, k1, k2tog, k11 (25 sts).

Row 10: Purl.

Row 11: K9, k2tog, k3, k2tog, k9 (23 sts).

Rows 12 to 18: Work 7 rows in st-st.

Rows 19 to 21: Work 3 rows in g-st, ending with a RS row.

Cast off in g-st.

HOOVES AND FOREARMS (make 2)

Using the long tail method and yarn D, cast on 6 sts.

Row 1: (Kfb) to end (12 sts).

Row 2: Purl.

Row 3: (Kfb, k1) to end (18 sts).

Row 4: K 1 row for fold line.

Rows 5 to 7: Beg with a k row, work 3 rows in st-st, ending on a k row.

Change to yarn A and dec:

Row 8: (P2tog, p1) to end (12 sts).

Rows 9 to 24: Work 16 rows in st-st.

Row 25: (K2tog, k1) to end (8 sts).

Break yarn, thread through sts on needle and leave loose.

BRACES (make 2)
Using the long tail method and yarn F, cast on 40 sts.
Row 1: Knit.
Cast off kwise.

HORNS (make 2)
Using the long tail method and yarn A, cast on 5 sts.
Rows 1 and 2: P 1 row then k 1 row.
Row 3: Change to yarn B and p 1 row.
Row 4: K1, (m1, k1) to end (9 sts).
Rows 5 and 6: P 1 row then k 1 row.
Break yarn and thread through sts on needle, pull tight and secure by threading yarn a second time through sts.

EARS (make 2)
Using the long tail method and yarn A, cast on 12 sts.
Rows 1 to 5: Beg with a p row, work 5 rows in st-st.
Row 6: (K2tog) to end (6 sts).
Row 7: Purl.
Break yarn and thread through sts on needle, pull tight and secure by threading yarn a second time through sts.

MANE
Using the long tail method and yarn D, cast on 22 sts and work in rev st-st.
Rows 1 to 3: Beg with a p row, rev st-st 3 rows.
Cast off kwise.

MAKING UP

Note: Sew up all row-end seams on right side using mattress stitch one stitch in from the edge, unless otherwise stated; a one-stitch seam allowance has been allowed for this.

BODY

Sew up side edges of wide part of body and, with this seam at centre back, oversew cast-on stitches. Stuff body and sew up side edges of neck and stuff neck leaving top of neck open.

HEAD

Gather round cast-on stitches of head, pull tight and secure. Sew up side edges leaving a gap. With seam at centre of underneath, sew across cast-off stitches. Stuff head and sew up gap. Pin and sew head to body with nose pointing down.

LEGS AND HOOVES

Gather round cast-on stitches of hooves, pull tight and secure. Sew up side edges of hooves and stuff hooves. Sew up side edges of legs and stuff. Pin legs to body, leaving a ¾in (2cm) gap at crotch, and sew in place.

TROUSERS

Place two pieces of trousers together matching all edges and sew up inside leg seams and across crotch. Sew up side seams and place trousers on Giraffe. Sew waist of trousers to row above waist of Giraffe using back stitch all the way round.

FOREARMS AND HOOVES

Gather round cast-on stitches of hooves, pull tight and secure. Sew up side edges of hooves and stuff hooves. Sew up side edges of forearms and stuff. Pull stitches on a thread tight and secure. Sew top of arms to 5th stripe of body in mustard.

BRACES AND BUTTONS

Place braces over top edge of waist of front of trousers at each side and sew in place. Take braces over shoulders, cross over, and sew ends to waist of trousers at back. Add two buttons to front of trousers.

HORNS

Sew up side edges of horns and sew to head.

EARS

Sew up side edges of ears and press flat. Fold cast-on stitches in half and sew together. Position ears, pin and sew ears to head.

MANE

Fold mane in half and oversew cast-on and cast-off stitches. Pin and sew mane to head.

FEATURES

Mark position of eyes with two pins and embroider eyes in black making a vertical chain stitch for each eye then a second chain stitch on top of first. Embroider nostrils and eyebrows in black using straight stitches (see page 155 for how to begin and fasten off invisibly for the embroidery).

MONKEY

INFORMATION YOU'LL NEED

MATERIALS

Any DK (US: light worsted) yarn
(amounts given are approximate)
Yarn A brown (20g for each Monkey)
Yarn B pale brown (10g)
Yarn C beige (10g)
Yarn D red (10g)
Yarn E pink (15g)
Oddment of black for embroidery
1 pair of 3.25mm (UK10:US3) needles and a spare needle of same size for dungarees
Knitters' pins and a blunt-ended needle for sewing up
Tweezers (optional)
Acrylic toy stuffing
2 small buttons for each Monkey

FINISHED SIZE

Monkey stands 8in (20.5cm) tall

TENSION

26 sts x 34 rows measure 4in (10cm) square over st-st using 3.25mm needles and DK yarn before stuffing.

ABBREVIATIONS

See page 156

HOW TO MAKE MONKEY

BODY

Using the long tail method and yarn A, cast on 28 sts.

Row 1: Purl.

Row 2: K1, (k6, m1, k1, m1, k6) twice, k1 (32 sts).

Rows 3 to 9: Work 7 rows in st-st.

Rows 10 and 11: Work 2 rows in g-st to mark waist.

Rows 12 to 23: Beg with a k row, work 12 rows in st-st.

Row 24: K1, (k6, k3tog, k6) twice, k1 (28 sts).

Row 25: Purl.

Row 26: K1, (k5, k3tog, k5) twice, k1 (24 sts).

Row 27: Purl.

Cast off.

HEAD

Using the long tail method and yarn A, cast on 24 sts.

Row 1: Purl.

Row 2: (Kfb, k2) to end (32 sts).

Rows 3 to 17: Work 15 rows in st-st.

Row 18: (K2tog, k2) to end (24 sts).

Row 19 and foll alt row: Purl.

Row 20: (K2tog, k1) to end (16 sts).

Row 22: (K2tog) to end (8 sts).

Break yarn and thread through sts on needle, pull tight and secure by threading yarn a second time through sts.

FACE PIECE

Using the long tail method and yarn B, cast on 10 sts.

Rows 1 to 5: Beg with a p row, work 5 rows in st-st.

Row 6: K1, k2tog, k4, k2tog, k1 (8 sts).

Row 7: Purl.

Row 8: (K2tog) to end (4 sts).

Break yarn and thread through sts on needle, pull tight and secure by threading yarn a second time through sts.

SNOUT

Using the long tail method and yarn C, cast on 24 sts.

Row 1: Purl.

Row 2: K2, (m1, k4) to last 2 sts, m1, k2 (30 sts).

Rows 3 to 5: Work 3 rows in st-st.

Row 6: K1, *k3, (k2tog) 4 times, k3; rep from * once, k1 (22 sts).

Row 7: Purl.

Row 8: K1, *k1, (k2tog) 4 times, k1; rep from * once, k1 (14 sts).

Cast off pwise.

LEGS (make 2)

Using the long tail method and yarn A, cast on 14 sts.

Rows 1 to 21: Beg with a p row, work 21 rows in st-st.

Cast off.

HANDS AND FOREARMS (make 2)

Using the long tail method and yarn A, cast on 10 sts.

Row 1: Purl.

Row 2: K1, m1, k8, m1, k1 (12 sts).

Rows 3 to 7: Work 5 rows in st-st.

Row 8: K1, m1, k10, m1, k1 (14 sts).

Rows 9 to 13: Work 5 rows in st-st.

Row 14: K1, m1, k12, m1, k1 (16 sts).

Rows 15 to 19: Work 5 rows in st-st.

Change to yarn B for hand and shape:

Row 20: K1, m1, k 14, m1, k1 (18 sts).

Rows 21 to 25: Work 5 rows in st-st.

Row 26: K6, cast off 6 sts, (7 sts now on RH needle), k to end (12 sts).

Rows 27 to 29: Push rem sts together and work 3 rows in st-st.
Row 30: (K2tog) to end (6 sts).
Break yarn and thread through sts on needle, pull tight and secure by threading yarn a second time through sts.

DUNGAREES
(make 2 pieces)

Note: Foll individual instructions as given for 1 front and 1 back of dungarees.

First leg
Using the long tail method and yarn D, cast on 12 sts and beg in g-st.
Rows 1 and 2: Work 2 rows in g-st.
Rows 3 and 4: K 1 row then p 1 row.
Break yarn and set aside.

Second leg
Work as for first leg but do not break yarn.

Join legs
Row 5: Beg with second leg and k10, k2tog, turn, using the knitting-on method cast on 5 sts, turn, then with the same yarn continue across first leg and k2tog, k to end (27 sts).
Rows 6 to 8: Beg with a p row, work 3 rows in st-st.
Row 9: K11, k2tog, k1, k2tog, k11 (25 sts).
Row 10: Purl.
Row 11: K9, k2tog, k3, k2tog, k9 (23 sts).
Rows 12 to 18: Work 7 rows in st-st.
Rows 19 to 21: Work 3 rows in g-st, ending with a RS row.
Cast off in g-st for back of dungarees or cont with bib for front of dungarees:

Divide for bib
Row 22: Cast off 7 sts kwise, k8 (9 sts now on RH needle), cast off rem 7 sts and fasten off.
Rejoin yarn to rem sts and patt:
****Row 23:** K2, (k1 tbl) 5 times, k2 (9 sts).
Row 24: K2, p5, k2.
Row 25: Knit.
Rows 26 to 31: Rep rows 24 and 25, 3 times more, ending with a k row.
Rows 32 and 33: Work 2 rows in g-st, ending with a RS row.
Cast off in g-st.

STRAPS FOR DUNGAREES
(make 2)

Using the long tail method and yarn D, cast on 24 sts.
Row 1: Knit.
Cast off kwise.

PINAFORE

Using the long tail method and yarn E, cast on 60 sts and beg in g-st.

Rows 1 and 2: Work 2 rows in g-st.

Rows 3 to 16: Beg with a k row, work 14 rows in st-st.

Row 17: (K2tog, k2) to end (45 sts).

Rows 18 and 19: Work 2 rows in g-st, ending with a RS row.

Divide for bib

Row 20: Cast off 18 sts kwise, k8 (9 sts now on RH needle), cast off rem 18 sts and fasten off.

Re-join yarn to rem sts and work bib from **, as for dungarees.

STRAPS FOR PINAFORE

Make straps using yarn E, as for dungarees.

FEET (make 2)

Using the long tail method and yarn B, cast on 9 sts.

Row 1: Purl.

Row 2: (Kfb) to end (18 sts).

Rows 3 to 7: Work 5 rows in st-st.

Row 8: K7, m1, k4, m1, k7 (20 sts).

Row 9: Purl.

Row 10: K7, cast off next 6 sts (8 sts now on RH needle), k6 (14 sts).

Rows 11 to 13: Push rem sts together and work 3 rows in st-st.

Row 14: (K2tog) to end (7 sts).

Break yarn and thread through sts on needle, pull tight and secure by threading yarn a second time through sts.

EARS (make 2)

Using the long tail method and yarn B, cast on 10 sts.

Row 1: Purl.

Row 2: K1, (m1, k2) to last st, m1, k1 (15 sts).

Rows 3 to 5: Work 3 rows in st-st.

Row 6: (K2tog, k1) to end (10 sts).

Row 7: (P2tog) to end (5 sts).

Break yarn and thread through sts on needle, pull tight and secure by threading yarn a second time through sts.

TAIL

Using the long tail method and yarn C, cast on 30 sts.

Rows 1 to 9: Beg with a p row, work 9 rows in st-st.

Cast off.

MAKING UP

Note: Sew up all row-end seams on right side using mattress stitch one stitch in from the edge, unless otherwise stated; a one-stitch seam allowance has been allowed for this.

BODY

Sew up side edges of body and with this seam at centre back, oversew cast-on stitches. Stuff body leaving neck open.

HEAD

Sew up side edges of head and stuff leaving neck open. Pin and sew head to body making a horizontal stitch over one stitch from head then a horizontal stitch over one stitch from body, and do this alternately all the way round.

SNOUT AND FACE PIECE

Sew up side edges of snout and with this seam at centre of underneath, sew across cast-off stitches. Stuff snout and arrange face piece and snout on face. Pin and sew in place.

LEGS

Sew up side edges of legs and stuff legs leaving ends open. Pin ends of legs to body, leaving a ¾in (2cm) gap at crotch, and sew in place.

HANDS AND FOREARMS

Fold cast-off stitches of thumbs in half, sew up and fasten off. Sew up side edges of arms, stuffing as you sew. Sew arms to Monkey.

DUNGAREES OR PINAFORE, STRAPS AND BUTTONS

Make up dungarees or pinafore, straps and buttons, as for Elephant on page 22.

FEET

Fold cast-off stitches of big toe in half, sew up and fasten off. Sew up side edges of feet and stuff feet and big toe with tweezers or tip of scissors. Fold cast-on stitches in half and oversew. Sew feet to ends of legs.

EARS

Sew up side edges of ears and with seam at centre back press flat. Pin and sew ears to head.

FEATURES

Mark position of eyes with two pins and embroider eyes in black making a vertical chain stitch for each eye then a second chain stitch on top of first. Embroider mouth in black with straight stitches and two short stitches for nostrils (see page 155 for how to begin and fasten off invisibly for the embroidery).

TAIL

Gather round one set of row ends, pull tight and secure. Sew cast-on edge to cast-off edge along the length of tail. Sew tail to back of Monkey below waistband sewing through trousers to body.

RHINO

INFORMATION YOU'LL NEED

MATERIALS

Any DK (US: light worsted) yarn (amounts given are approximate)
Yarn A dark grey (20g)
Yarn B forest green (10g)
Oddment of black for embroidery
1 pair of 3.25mm (UK10:US3) needles and a spare needle of same size
Knitters' pins and a blunt-ended needle for sewing up
Tweezers (optional)
Acrylic toy stuffing
2 small buttons

FINISHED SIZE

Rhino stands 7½in (19cm) tall

TENSION

26 sts x 34 rows measure 4in (10cm) square over st-st using 3.25mm needles and DK yarn before stuffing.

ABBREVIATIONS

See page 156

HOW TO MAKE RHINO

BODY

Make body using yarn A, as for Elephant on page 18.

HEAD

Make head using yarn A, as for Hippo on page 26.

MUZZLE

Using the long tail method and yarn A, cast on 32 sts.

Rows 1 to 5: Beg with a p row, work 5 rows in st-st.

Row 6: K1, (k6, k3tog, k6) twice, k1 (28 sts).

Rows 7 to 11: Work 5 rows in st-st.

Row 12: K1, (k5, k3tog, k5) twice, k1 (24 sts).

Rows 13 to 17: Work 5 rows in st-st.

Row 18: K1, (k4, k3tog, k4) twice, k1 (20 sts).

Row 19: K 1 row for fold line.

Rows 20 and 21: K 1 row then p 1 row.

Row 22: (K2tog) to end (10 sts).

Row 23: Purl.

Row 24: (K2tog) to end (5 sts).

Break yarn and thread through sts on needle, pull tight and secure by threading yarn a second time through sts.

LEGS (make 2)

Make legs using yarn A, as for Hippo on page 26.

ARMS (make 2)

Using the long tail method and yarn A, cast on 12 sts.

Row 1: Purl.

Row 2: (K1, m1, k4, m1, k1) twice (16 sts).

Rows 3 to 9: Work 7 rows in st-st.

Row 10: K6, (k2tog) twice, k6 (14 sts).

Row 11: Purl.

Row 12: K6, k2tog, k6 (13 sts).

Rows 13 to 23: Work 11 rows in st-st.

Row 24: K1, (k2tog, k1) to end (9 sts).

Break yarn and thread through sts on needle, and leave loose.

DUNGAREES AND STRAPS

Make dungarees and straps using yarn B, as for Hippo on page 28.

EARS (make 2)

Using the long tail method and yarn A, cast on 12 sts.
Rows 1 to 5: Beg with a p row, work 5 rows in st-st.
Row 6: (K2tog) to end (6 sts).
Row 7: Purl.
Break yarn and thread through sts on needle, pull tight and secure by threading yarn a second time through sts.

HORN

Using the long tail method and yarn A, cast on 18 sts.
Rows 1 to 3: Beg with a p row, work 3 rows in st-st.
Row 4: (K2tog, k1) to end (12 sts).
Rows 5 to 7: Work 3 rows in st-st.
Row 8: (K2tog) to end (6 sts).
Row 9: Purl.
Break yarn and thread through sts on needle, pull tight and secure by threading yarn a second time through sts.

MAKING UP

Note: Sew up all row-end seams on right side using mattress stitch one stitch in from the edge, unless otherwise stated; a one-stitch seam allowance has been allowed for this.

BODY

Sew up side edges of body and with this seam at centre back, oversew cast-on stitches. Stuff body leaving neck open.

HEAD AND MUZZLE

Sew up side edges of head and stuff head leaving neck open. Sew lower edge of head to body making a horizontal stitch from head then a horizontal stitch from body, and do this alternately all the way round. Sew up side edges of muzzle and stuff muzzle. Pin and sew muzzle to Rhino.

LEGS AND ARMS

Make up legs and arms, as for Hippo on page 30.

DUNGAREES, STRAPS AND BUTTONS

Make up dungarees, straps and buttons, as for Elephant on page 22.

EARS

Sew up side edges of ears and press flat. Fold cast-on edge in half and pin and sew ears to Rhino.

FEATURES

Mark position of eyes with two pins above muzzle and embroider eyes in black making a vertical chain stitch for each eye then a second chain stitch on top of first. Embroider eyebrows in black using straight stitches (see page 155 for how to begin and fasten off invisibly for the embroidery).

HORN

Sew up side edges of horn and stuff with tweezers or tip of scissors. Pin and sew horn to muzzle.

ANTEATER

INFORMATION YOU'LL NEED

MATERIALS

Any DK (US: light worsted) yarn
(amounts given are approximate)
Yarn A brown (20g)
Yarn B black (5g)
Yarn C white (5g)
Yarn D pale brown (15g)
Yarn E claret (10g)
Oddment of black for embroidery
1 pair of 3.25mm (UK10:US3) needles and a spare needle of same size for dungarees
Knitters' pins and a blunt-ended needle for sewing up
Acrylic toy stuffing
2 small buttons

FINISHED SIZE

Anteater stands 7in (18cm) tall

TENSION

26 sts x 34 rows measure 4in (10cm) square over st-st using 3.25mm needles and DK yarn before stuffing.

ABBREVIATIONS

See page 156

SPECIAL ABBREVIATION

w1: wrap 1 stitch – take yarn between needles to opposite side, slip 1 stitch pwise from LH needle to RH needle, then take yarn between needles to first side.

HOW TO MAKE ANTEATER

BODY AND HEAD

Using the long tail method and yarn A, cast on 36 sts.
Row 1: Purl.
Row 2: K1, (k8, m1, k1, m1, k8) twice, k1 (40 sts).
Rows 3 to 9: Beg with a p row, work 7 rows in st-st.
Rows 10 and 11: Work 2 rows in g-st to mark waist.
Rows 12 to 15: Beg with a k row, work 4 rows in st-st.
Row 16: K1, (k8, k3tog, k8) twice, k1 (36 sts).
Row 17: Purl.
Row 18: K10, w1 (see special abbreviation), turn.
Row 19: S1p, p to end.
Row 20: K8, w1, turn.
Row 21: S1p, p to end.
Row 22: K6, w1, turn.
Row 23: S1p, p to end.
Row 24: Knit.
Row 25: P10, w1, turn.
Row 26: S1k, k to end.
Row 27: P8, w1, turn.
Row 28: S1k, k to end.
Row 29: P6, w1, turn.
Row 30: S1k, k to end.
Row 31: Purl.
Change to yarn B and dec:
Row 32: K1, (k7, k3tog, k7) twice, k1 (32 sts).
Rows 33 to 37: Beg with a p row, work 5 rows in st-st.
Rows 38 and 39: Change to yarn C and work 2 rows in st-st.
Rows 40 to 51: Change to yarn D and work 12 rows in st-st.
Row 52: (K2tog, k2) to end (24 sts).
Row 53 and foll alt row: Purl.
Row 54: (K2tog, k1) to end (16 sts).
Row 56: (K2tog) to end (8 sts).
Break yarn and thread through sts on needle, pull tight and secure by threading yarn a second time through sts.

PROBOSCIS

Using the long tail method and yarn B, cast on 8 sts.
Row 1: Purl.
Row 2: (Kfb, k1) to end (12 sts).
Rows 3 to 5: Beg with a p row, work 3 rows in st-st.
Rows 6 to 9: Change to yarn D and work 4 rows in st-st.
Row 10: K1, m1, k to last st, m1, k1 (14 sts).
Rows 11 to 13: Work 3 rows in st-st.
Rows 14 to 29: Work rows 10 to 13, 4 times more (22 sts)
Rows 30 and 31: Cast off 4 sts at beg of next 2 rows (14 sts).
Row 32: K2tog, k to last 2 sts, k2tog (12 sts).
Row 33: Purl.
Rows 34 to 37: Rep rows 32 and 33, twice more (8 sts).
Row 38: (K2tog) to end (4 sts).
Break yarn and thread through sts on needle, pull tight and secure by threading yarn a second time through sts.

FEET AND LEGS (make 2)

Using the long tail method and yarn A, cast on 16 sts.
Row 1: Purl.
Row 2: (K1, kfb) 4 times, (kfb, k1) 4 times (24 sts).
Rows 3 to 9: Work 7 rows in st-st.
Row 10: K6, (k2tog) 6 times, k6 (18 sts).
Row 11: Purl.
Row 12: K7, (k2tog) twice, k7 (16 sts).
Rows 13 to 17: Work 5 rows in st-st.
Cast off.

HANDS AND FOREARMS (make 2)

Using the long tail method and yarn C, cast on 8 sts.
Row 1 and foll alt row: Purl.
Row 2: (Kfb) to end (16 sts).
Row 4: (Kfb, k3) to end (20 sts).
Rows 5 to 7: Work 3 rows in st-st.
Join on yarn A and dec:
Row 8: (K2tog, k2) to end (15 sts).
Rows 9 to 11: Work 3 rows in st-st.
Rows 12 to 17: Change to yarn C and work 6 rows in st-st.
Row 18: (K2tog, k1) to end (10 sts).
Break yarn, thread through sts on needle and leave loose.

DUNGAREES (make 2 pieces)

Note: Foll individual instructions as given for 1 front and 1 back of dungarees.

First leg

Using the long tail method and yarn E, cast on 12 sts and beg in g-st.

Rows 1 and 2: Work 2 rows in g-st.

Break yarn and set aside.

Second leg

Work as for first leg but do not break yarn.

Join legs

Row 3: Beg with second leg and k10, k2tog, turn, using the knitting-on method cast on 5 sts, turn, then with the same yarn continue across first leg and k2tog, k to end (27 sts).

Row 4 and foll 2 alt rows: Purl.

Row 5: K2, m1, k23, m1, k2 (29 sts).

Row 7: K12, k2tog, k1, k2tog, k12 (27 sts).

Row 9: K10, k2tog, k3, k2tog, k10 (25 sts).

Rows 10 to 14: Work 5 rows in st-st.

Rows 15 to 17: Work 3 rows in g-st, ending with a RS row.

Cast off in g-st for back of dungarees or cont with bib for front of dungarees:

Divide for bib

Row 18: Cast off 6 sts kwise, k12 (13 sts now on RH needle), cast off rem 6 sts and fasten off.

Rejoin yarn to rem sts and patt:

Row 19: K2, (k1 tbl) 9 times, k2 (13 sts).

Row 20: K2, p9, k2.

Row 21: Knit.

Rows 22 to 27: Rep rows 20 and 21, 3 times more, ending with a k row.

Rows 28 and 29: Work 2 rows in g-st, ending with a RS row.

Cast off in g-st.

STRAPS FOR DUNGAREES (make 2)

Using the long tail method and yarn E, cast on 26 sts.

Row 1: Knit.

Cast off kwise.

EARS (make 2)

Using the long tail method and yarn D, cast on 6 sts.

Row 1: Purl.

Row 2: (K1, m1) twice, k2, (m1, k1) twice (10 sts).

Rows 3 and 4: P 1 row then k 1 row.

Row 5: P2, (p2tog, p2) twice (8 sts).

Break yarn and thread through sts on needle, pull tight and secure by threading yarn a second time through sts.

TAIL

Using the long tail method and yarn A, cast on 15 sts loosely.

Row 1: K1, *k next st placing index finger of LH behind RH needle and wind yarn round finger and needle clockwise 3 times, then wind just round needle in the same direction once, knit st pulling 4 loops through, place these loops on LH needle and k into the back of them, pull on loops just made to secure, rep from * to last st, k1.

Row 2: Knit.

Row 3: P13, w1 (see special abbreviation), turn.

Row 4: S1k, k to end.

Row 5: P10, w1, turn.

Row 6: S1k, k to end.

Row 7: P7, w1, turn.

Row 8: S1k, k to end.

Row 9: P10, w1, turn.

Row 10: S1k, k to end.

Row 11: P13, w1, turn.

Row 12: S1k, k to end.

Row 13: Purl.

Cast off.

MAKING UP

Note: Sew up all row-end seams on right side using mattress stitch one stitch in from the edge, unless otherwise stated; a one-stitch seam allowance has been allowed for this.

BODY AND HEAD

Sew up side edges of head and body leaving a gap. With this seam at centre back, oversew cast-on stitches. Stuff head and body and sew up gap.

PROBOSCIS

Sew up side edges of proboscis from tip to cast-off stitches. Stuff then pin and sew proboscis to head.

FEET AND LEGS

Fold cast-on stitches of feet in half and oversew. Sew up side edges of legs and stuff feet and legs. Pin legs to body, leaving a ¾in (2cm) gap at crotch, and sew in place.

HANDS AND FOREARMS

Gather round cast-on stitches of forearms, pull tight and secure. Sew up side edges of forearms and stuff. Pull stitches on a thread tight and secure. Sew forearms to Anteater at both sides.

DUNGAREES, STRAPS AND BUTTONS

Make up dungarees, straps and buttons, as for Elephant on page 22.

EARS

Sew up side edges of ears and press flat. Position ears and sew to head.

FEATURES

Mark position of eyes with two pins and embroider eyes in black making a vertical chain stitch for each eye then a second chain stitch on top of first. Embroider eyebrows in black using straight stitches (see page 155 for how to begin and fasten off invisibly for the embroidery).

TAIL

Fold tail and oversew cast-on and cast-off stitches. Stuff tail with tweezers or tip of scissors and sew tail to back of Anteater.

FLAMINGO

INFORMATION YOU'LL NEED

MATERIALS

Any DK (US: light worsted) yarn (amounts given are approximate)
Yarn A pale pink (20g)
Yarn B cerise (10g)
Yarn C white (5g)
Yarn D black (5g)
Yarn E medium pink (5g)
Oddment of black for embroidery
1 pair of 3.25mm (UK10:US3) needles
Knitters' pins and a blunt-ended needle for sewing up
Tweezers (optional)
Acrylic toy stuffing
Thick cardboard
6 chenille stems
2 small buttons

FINISHED SIZE

Flamingo stands 11in (28cm) tall

TENSION

26 sts x 34 rows measure 4in (10cm) square over st-st using 3.25mm needles and DK yarn before stuffing.

ABBREVIATIONS

See page 156

SPECIAL ABBREVIATION

w1: wrap 1 stitch – take yarn between needles to opposite side, slip 1 stitch pwise from LH needle to RH needle, then take yarn between needles to first side.

HOW TO MAKE FLAMINGO

BODY, TAIL, NECK AND HEAD

Using the long tail method and yarn A, cast on 8 sts.

Row 1 and foll 4 alt rows: Purl.
Row 2: (Kfb) to end (16 sts).
Row 4: (Kfb, k1) to end (24 sts).
Row 6: (Kfb, k2) to end (32 sts).
Row 8: (Kfb, k3) to end (40 sts).
Row 10: (Kfb, k4) to end (48 sts).
Rows 11 to 21: Work 11 rows in st-st.
Rows 22 and 23: Work 2 rows in g-st to mark waist.
Rows 24 to 27: Beg with a k row, work 4 rows in st-st.

Shape tail

Row 28: K8, w1 (see special abbreviation), turn.
Row 29: S1p, p to end.
Row 30: K6, w1, turn.
Row 31: S1p, p to end.
Row 32: K4, w1, turn.
Row 33: S1p, p to end.
Row 34: Knit.
Row 35: P8, w1, turn.
Row 36: S1k, k to end.
Row 37: P6, w1, turn.
Row 38: S1k, k to end.
Row 39: P4, w1, turn.
Row 40: S1k, k to end.
Row 41: P13, (p2tog, p2) 6 times, p11 (42 sts).
Row 42: Cast off 8 sts kwise, k25, (26 sts now on RH needle), cast off rem 8 sts and fasten off.

Rejoin yarn and shape:

Row 43: P2tog, p to last 2 sts, p2tog (24 sts).
Row 44: K2tog, k6, (k2tog) 4 times, k6, k2tog (18 sts).
Row 45: P2tog, p to last 2 sts, p2tog (16 sts).
Rows 46 to 61: Work 16 rows in st-st.

Shape head

Row 62: K1, m1, k4, w1, turn.
Row 63: S1p, p to end (17 sts).
Row 64: Knit.
Row 65: P1, m1, p4, w1, turn.
Row 66: S1k, k to end (18 sts).
Row 67: Purl.
Row 68: K1, m1, k5, w1, turn.
Row 69: S1p, p to end (19 sts).
Row 70: Knit.
Row 71: P1, m1, p5, w1, turn.
Row 72: S1k, k to end (20 sts).
Row 73: Purl.
Row 74: K1, m1, k6, w1, turn.
Row 75: S1p, p to end (21 sts).
Row 76: Knit.
Row 77: P1, m1, p6, w1, turn.
Row 78: S1k, k to end (22 sts).
Row 79: Purl.
Row 80: K1, m1, k7, w1, turn.
Row 81: S1p, p to end (23 sts).
Row 82: Knit.
Row 83: P1, m1, p7, w1, turn.
Row 84: S1k, k to end (24 sts).
Rows 85 to 89: Work 5 rows in st-st.
Row 90: (K2tog, k1) to end (16 sts).
Row 91: Purl.
Row 92: (K2tog) to end (8 sts).

Break yarn and thread through sts on needle, pull tight and secure by threading yarn a second time through sts.

DUNGAREES

Using the long tail method and yarn B, cast on 8 sts.

Row 1 and foll 5 alt rows: Purl.
Row 2: (Kfb) to end (16 sts).
Row 4: As row 2 (32 sts).
Row 6: (Kfb, k3) to end (40 sts).
Row 8: (Kfb, k4) to end (48 sts).
Row 10: (Kfb, k5) to end (56 sts).
Row 12: (Kfb, k6) to end (64 sts).
Rows 13 to 21: Beg with a p row, work 9 rows in st-st.
Rows 22 to 24: Work 3 rows in g-st, ending with a RS row.

Divide for bib

Row 25: Cast off 25 sts kwise, k13 (14 sts now on RH needle), cast off rem 25 sts kwise and fasten off.

Re-join yarn to rem sts and patt:

Row 26: K2, (k1 tbl) 10 times, k2 (14 sts).
Row 27: K2, p10, k2.
Row 28: Knit.
Rows 29 to 32: Rep rows 27 and 28 twice more, ending with a k row.
Rows 33 and 34: Work 2 rows in g-st ending with a RS row.

Cast off in g-st.

BEAK

Using the long tail method and yarn C, cast on 13 sts.

Rows 1 to 3: Beg with a p row, work 3 rows in st-st.

Row 4: K10, w1, turn.

Row 5: S1p, p6, w1, turn.

Row 6: S1k, k to end.

Row 7: Purl.

Rows 8 to 23: Rep rows 4 to 7, 4 times more.

Rows 24 to 29: Change to yarn D and work 6 rows in st-st.

Row 30: K1, (k2tog, k1) to end (9 sts).

Break yarn and thread through sts on needle, pull tight and secure by threading yarn a second time through sts.

LEGS (make 2)

Using the long tail method and yarn A, cast on 10 sts.

Rows 1 to 15: Beg with a p row, work 15 rows in st-st.

Rows 16 and 17: P 1 row then k 1 row.

Rows 18 to 25: Beg with a k row, work 8 rows in st-st.

Rows 26 to 29: Change to yarn B and work 4 rows in g-st.

Rows 30 to 33: Beg with a k row, work 4 rows in st-st.

Cast off.

FEET (make 2)

Using the long tail method and yarn E, cast on 15 sts.

Rows 1 to 3: Beg with a p row, work 3 rows in st-st.

Row 4: K3, k2tog, k5, k2tog, k3 (13 sts).

Rows 5 to 7: Work 3 rows in st-st.

Row 8: K3, k2tog, k3, k2tog, k3 (11 sts).

Rows 9 to 11: Work 3 rows in st-st.

Row 12: K2, k2tog, k3, k2tog, k2 (9 sts).

Row 13: Purl.

Row 14: K2, k2tog, k1, k2tog, k2 (7 sts).

Break yarn and thread through sts on needle, pull tight and secure by threading yarn a second time through sts.

WINGS (make 2)

Using the long tail method and yarn E, cast on 14 sts.
Row 1: Purl.
Row 2: K2, (m1, k2) to end (20 sts).
Rows 3 to 9: Work 7 rows in st-st.
Row 10: (K2tog, k6, k2tog) twice (16 sts).
Row 11 and foll alt row: Purl.
Row 12: (K2tog, k4, k2tog) twice (12 sts).
Row 14: (K2tog, k2, k2tog) twice (8 sts).
Row 15: Purl.
Row 16: (K2tog) to end (4 sts).
Break yarn and thread through sts on needle, pull tight and secure by threading yarn a second time through sts.

STRAPS (make 2)

Using the long tail method and yarn B, cast on 20 sts.
Row 1: Knit.
Cast off kwise.

MAKING UP

Note: Sew up all row-end seams on right side using mattress stitch one stitch in from the edge, unless otherwise stated; a one-stitch seam allowance has been allowed for this.

BODY, TAIL, NECK AND HEAD

Gather round cast-on stitches of body, pull tight and secure. Sew up side edges of head and neck and stuff head, then lightly stuff neck. Sew around tail and body leaving a gap, stuff and sew up gap.

DUNGAREES

Sew up side edges of dungarees and place on Flamingo. Sew top edge of dungarees to waist of body using back stitch all the way round.

BEAK

Sew up side edges of beak. Stuff beak and pin and sew beak to head.

LEGS

Place three chenille stems together and place on wrong side of leg and sew up side edges of leg enclosing the chenille stems inside. Cut chenille stems to length of leg. Repeat for other leg and sew legs to underneath of Flamingo, sewing through dungarees to body. Bend legs.

FEET

Sew up side edges of feet and place inside a triangle of thick cardboard measuring 1in (2.5cm) on narrow edge and 1¼in (3cm) on tall sides. Oversew across cast-on stitches of feet and sew feet to ends of legs.

WINGS

Fold wings and oversew side edges. Sew wings to Flamingo at each side.

STRAPS AND BUTTONS

Sew straps to each side of bib, take straps over back, cross over and sew ends of straps to top of dungarees. Add two buttons to bib.

FEATURES

Mark position of eyes with two pins and embroider eyes in black making a chain stitch for each eye and a second chain stitch on top of first (see page 155 for how to begin and fasten off invisibly for the embroidery).

WEAVER BIRD

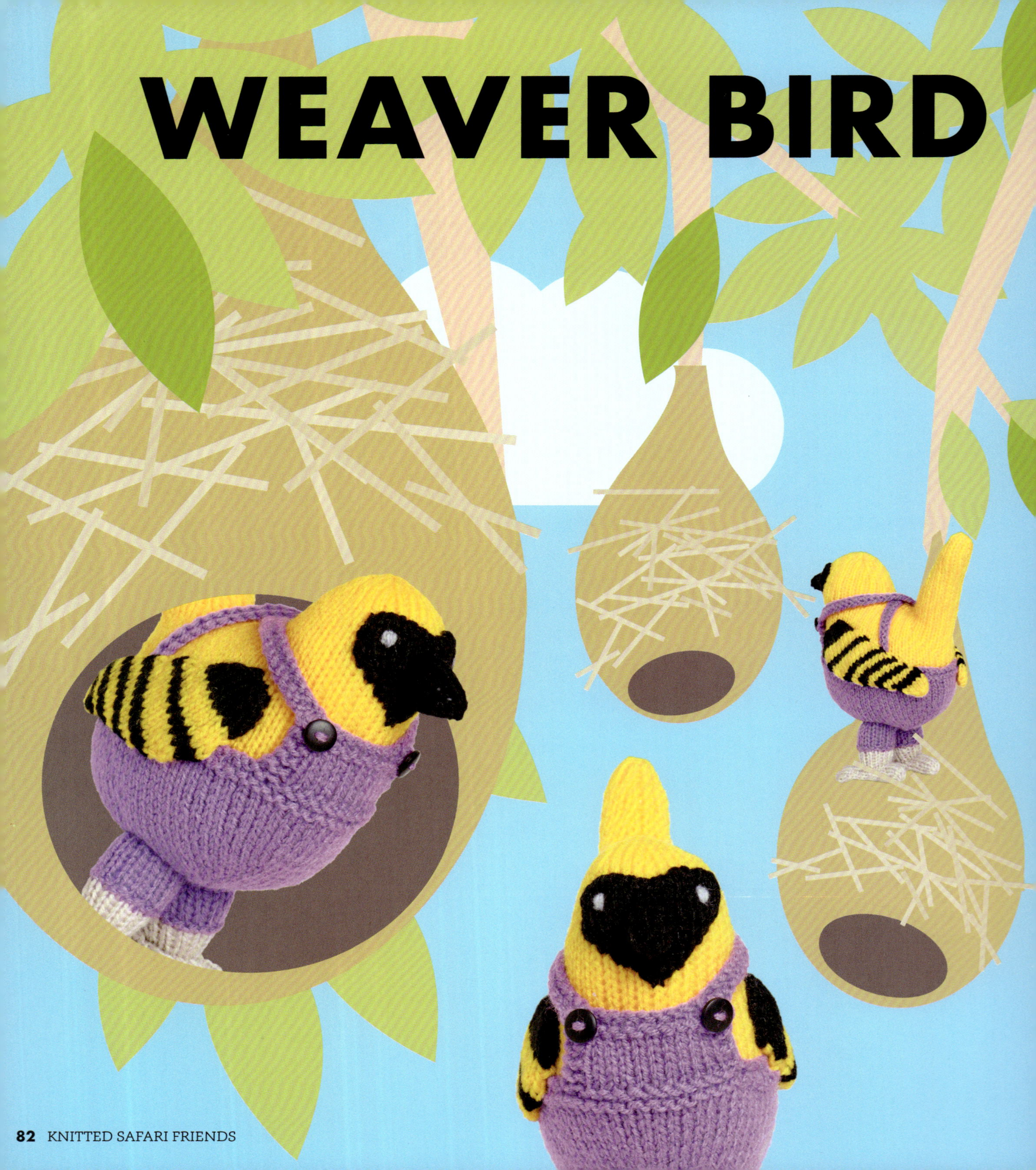

INFORMATION YOU'LL NEED

MATERIALS

Any DK (US: light worsted) yarn
(amounts given are approximate)
Yarn A gold (20g)
Yarn B lavender (10g)
Yarn C silver grey (5g)
Yarn D black (5g)
Oddment of silver grey for embroidery
1 pair of 3.25mm (UK10:US3) needles
Knitters' pins and a blunt-ended needle for sewing up
Tweezers (optional)
Acrylic toy stuffing
Small piece of thick cardboard
2 small buttons

FINISHED SIZE

Weaver Bird stands 8in (20.5cm) tall

TENSION

26 sts x 34 rows measure 4in (10cm) square over st-st using 3.25mm needles and DK yarn before stuffing.

ABBREVIATIONS

See page 156

SPECIAL ABBREVIATION

w1: wrap 1 stitch – take yarn between needles to opposite side, slip 1 stitch pwise from LH needle to RH needle, then take yarn between needles to first side.

HOW TO MAKE WEAVER BIRD

BODY, HEAD AND TAIL

Using the long tail method and yarn A, cast on 22 sts.

Row 1 and foll 5 alt rows: Purl.

Row 2: K2, (m1, k2) to end (32 sts).

Row 4: *(K2, m1) twice, k8, (m1, k2) twice; rep from * once (40 sts).

Row 6: *(K2, m1) twice, k12, (m1, k2) twice; rep from * once (48 sts).

Row 8: *K2, m1, k20, m1, k2; rep from * once (52 sts).

Row 10: *K2, m1, k22, m1, k2; rep from * once (56 sts).

Row 12: *K2, m1, k24, m1, k2; rep from * once (60 sts).

Rows 13 to 19: Work 7 rows in st-st.

Rows 20 and 21: Work 2 rows in g-st to mark waist.

Rows 22 to 25: Work 4 rows in st-st.

Row 26: K56, w1 (see special abbreviation), turn.

Row 27: S1p, p52, w1, turn.

Row 28: S1k, k to end.

Row 29: P54, w1, turn.

Row 30: S1k, k48, w1, turn.

Row 31: S1p, p to end.

Row 32: K52, w1, turn.

Row 33: S1p, p44, w1, turn.

Row 34: S1k, k to end.

Row 35: P50, w1, turn.

Row 36: S1k, k40, w1, turn.

Row 37: S1p, p to end.

Row 38: K10, cast off 3 sts, k33, turn.

Row 39: P34, turn and work on these 34 sts.

Row 40: k2tog, k to last 2 sts, k2tog (32 sts).

Rows 41 to 47: Work 7 rows in st-st.

Row 48: (K2tog, k2) to end (24 sts).

Row 49 and foll alt row: Purl.

Row 50: (K2tog, k1) to end (16 sts).

Row 52: (K2tog) to end (8 sts).

Break yarn and thread through sts on needle, pull tight and secure by threading yarn a second time through sts.

Row 53: Rejoin yarn to rem sts halfway along row cast off 3 sts, k to end.

Row 54: Push rem sts together and p 1 row (20 sts).

Rows 55 to 64: Work 10 rows in st-st.

Row 65: K8, (k2tog) twice, k8 (18 sts).

Rows 66 to 68: Work 3 rows in st-st.

Row 69: K7, (k2tog) twice, k7 (16 sts).

Rows 70 to 72: Work 3 rows in st-st.

Row 73: K6, (k2tog) twice, k6 (14 sts).

Rows 74 to 76: Work 3 rows in st-st.

Row 77: K5, (k2tog) twice, k5 (12 sts).

Rows 78 to 80: Work 3 rows in st-st.

Cast off.

DUNGAREES

Using the long tail method and yarn B, cast on 22 sts.

Row 1 and foll 6 alt rows: Purl.

Row 2: K2, (m1, k2) to end (32 sts).

Row 4: *(K2, m1) twice, k8, (m1, k2) twice; rep from * once (40 sts).

Row 6: *(K2, m1) twice, k12, (m1, k2) twice; rep from * once (48 sts).

Row 8: *(K2, m1) twice, k16, (m1, k2) twice; rep from * once (56 sts).

Row 10: *(K2, m1) twice, k20, (m1, k2) twice; rep from * once (64 sts).

Row 12: *K2, m1, k28, m1, k2; rep from * once (68 sts).

Row 14: *K2, m1, k30, m1, k2; rep from * once (72 sts).

Rows 15 to 21: Work 7 rows in st-st.

Rows 22 to 24: Work 3 rows in g-st, ending with a RS row.

Divide for bib

Row 25: Cast off 29 sts kwise, k13 (14 sts now on RH needle), cast off rem 29 sts and fasten off.

Rejoin yarn to rem sts and patt:

Row 26: K2, (k1 tbl) 10 times, k2 (14 sts).

Row 27: K2, p10, k2.

Row 28: Knit.

Rows 29 to 32: Rep rows 27 and 28 twice more, ending with a k row.

Rows 33 and 34: Work 2 rows in g-st, ending with a RS row.

Cast off in g-st.

STRAPS FOR DUNGAREES (make 2)

Using the long tail method and yarn B, cast on 32 sts.

Row 1: Knit.

Cast off kwise.

LEGS (make 2)

Using the long tail method and yarn C, cast on 7 sts.

Row 1: Purl.

Row 2: (Kfb) to end (14 sts).

Rows 3 to 7: Work 5 rows in st-st.

Row 8: Change to yarn B and k 1 row.

Row 9: K4, (kfb, k4) twice (16 sts).

Rows 10 to 15: Work 6 rows in st-st.

Cast off.

FEET AND BACK TOE (make 2)

Using the long tail method and yarn C, cast on 15 sts.

Rows 1 to 3: Beg with a p row, work 3 rows in st-st.

Row 4: K3, k2tog, k5, k2tog, k3 (13 sts).

Rows 5 to 7: Work 3 rows in st-st.

Row 8: K3, k2tog, k3, k2tog, k3 (11 sts).

Rows 9 to 11: Work 3 rows in st-st.

Row 12: K2, k2tog, k3, k2tog, k2 (9 sts).

Rows 13 to 15: Work 3 rows in st-st.

Break yarn and thread through sts on needle, pull tight and secure by threading yarn a second time through sts.

TOES (make 6)

Using the long tail method and yarn C, cast on 8 sts.

Rows 1 to 3: Beg with a p row, work 3 rows in st-st.

Break yarn and thread through sts on needle, pull tight and secure by threading yarn a second time through sts.

WINGS (make 2)

Using the long tail method and yarn D, cast on 9 sts.

Row 1 and foll alt row: Purl.

Row 2: K1, m1, k3, m1, k1, m1, k3, m1, k1 (13 sts).

Row 4: K1, m1, k5, m1, k1, m1, k5, m1, k1 (17 sts).

Row 5: Purl.

Join on yarn A and work in stripes, carrying yarn loosely up side of work:

Row 6: Yarn A-k8, m1, k1, m1, k8 (19 sts).

Row 7 and foll alt row: Purl.

Row 8: K9, m1, k1, m1, k9 (21 sts).

Row 10: Yarn D-k10, m1, k1, m1 k10 (23 sts).

Row 11: Purl.

Row 12: Yarn A-k2tog, k9, m1, k1, m1, k9, k2tog (23 sts).

Row 13: Purl.

Rows 14 and 15: Rep rows 12 and 13 once.

Row 16: Yarn D-k2tog, k9, m1, k1, m1, k9, k2tog (23 sts).

Row 17: Purl.

Row 18: Yarn A-(k2tog) twice, k7, m1, k1, m1, k7, (k2tog) twice (21 sts).

Row 19: Purl.

Row 20: Yarn D-(k2tog) twice, k6, m1, k1, m1, k6, (k2tog) twice (19 sts).

Row 21: Purl.

Row 22: Yarn A-(k2tog) twice, k5, m1, k1, m1, k5, (k2tog) twice (17 sts).

Row 23: Purl.

Row 24: Yarn D-(k2tog) twice, k4, m1, k1, m1, k4, (k2tog) twice (15 sts).

Row 25: Purl.

Row 26: Yarn A-(k2tog) twice, k3, m1, k1, m1, k3, (k2tog) twice (13 sts).

Row 27: Purl.

Row 28: Yarn D-(k2tog) twice, k2, m1, k1, m1, k2, (k2tog) twice (11 sts).

Row 29: Purl.

Row 30: Yarn A-k2tog, k7, k2tog (9 sts).

Row 31: Purl.

Row 32: K2tog, k5, k2tog (7 sts).

Row 33: Purl.

Break yarn and thread through sts on needle, pull tight and secure by threading yarn a second time through sts.

FACE PATCH

Using the long tail method and yarn D, cast on 3 sts.

Row 1 and foll 5 alt rows: Purl.

Row 2: K1, m1, k1, m1, k1 (5 sts).

Row 4: K1, m1, k3, m1, k1 (7 sts).

Row 6: (K1, m1) twice, k3, (m1, k1) twice (11 sts).

Row 8: K1, m1, k9, m1, k1 (13 sts).

Row 10: (K1, m1) twice, k9, (m1, k1) twice (17 sts).

Row 12: K7, turn.

Row 13: S1p, p to end.

Row 14: Knit.

Row 15: P7, turn.

Row 16: S1k, k to end.

Row 17: (P2tog) twice, p9, (p2tog) twice (13 sts).

Cast off.

BEAK

Using the long tail method and yarn D, cast on 10 sts.

Rows 1 to 3: Beg with a p row, work 3 rows in st-st.

Row 4: K3, (k2tog) twice, k3 (8 sts).

Rows 5 to 7: Work 3 rows in st-st.

Row 8: K1, (k2tog) 3 times, k1 (5 sts).

Break yarn and thread through sts on needle, pull tight and secure by threading yarn a second time through sts.

MAKING UP

Note: Sew up all row-end seams on right side using mattress stitch one stitch in from the edge, unless otherwise stated; a one-stitch seam allowance has been allowed for this.

BODY, HEAD AND TAIL

Sew up side edges of head, sew across back and side edges down to cast-on stitches. Stuff head and body. Fold cast-on stitches in half and oversew.

DUNGAREES, STRAPS AND BUTTONS

Fold cast-on stitches of dungarees in half and oversew. Sew up side edges of dungarees and place on Weaver Bird. Sew waist of dungarees to waist of Weaver Bird using back stitch all the way round. Sew ends of straps to bib, take straps over shoulders, cross over and sew to sides. Add two buttons to bib.

LEGS

Sew up side edges of legs and stuff legs. Sew legs to underneath of Weaver Bird sewing through dungarees to body.

FEET AND TOES

Sew up side edges of back toe of foot and stuff back toe with a tiny bit of stuffing, with tweezers or tip of scissors. Finish sewing up side edges and place inside a triangle of thick cardboard measuring 1in (2.5cm) on narrow edge and 1¼in (3cm) on tall sides. Oversew cast-on stitches enclosing cardboard inside. Sew up side edges of each toe and sew a toe to middle of each foot and two more either side at front. Sew feet to ends of legs.

WINGS

Fold wings and oversew open edges. Pin and sew wings to Weaver Bird at each side.

FACE PATCH AND BEAK

Pin face patch to face and sew in place around outside edge. Sew up side edges of beak and stuff with tweezers or tip of scissors. Pin and sew beak to head.

FEATURES

Mark position of eyes with two pins and embroider eyes in silver grey making a vertical chain stitch for each eye then a second chain stitch on top of first (see page 155 for how to begin and fasten off invisibly for the embroidery).

SLOTH

INFORMATION YOU'LL NEED

Any DK (US: light worsted) yarn
(amounts given are approximate)
Yarn A pale brown (15g for each Sloth)
Yarn B cream (5g)
Yarn C dark brown (5g)
Yarn D black (5g)
Yarn E blue (10g)
Yarn F purple (15g)
Oddments of black and dark brown for embroidery
1 pair of 3.25mm (UK10:US3) needles and a spare needle of same size for dungarees
Knitters' pins and a blunt-ended needle for sewing up
Acrylic toy stuffing
2 small buttons for each Sloth

FINISHED SIZE

Sloth stands 8¼in (21cm) tall

TENSION

26 sts x 34 rows measure 4in (10cm) square over st-st using 3.25mm needles and DK yarn before stuffing.

ABBREVIATIONS

See page 156

HOW TO MAKE SLOTH

BODY

Using the long tail method and yarn A, cast on 28 sts.

Row 1: Purl.

Row 2: K1, (k6, m1, k1, m1, k6) twice, k1 (32 sts).

Rows 3 to 9: Work 7 rows in st-st.

Rows 10 and 11: Work 2 rows in g-st to mark waist.

Rows 12 to 23: Beg with a k row, work 12 rows in st-st.

Row 24: K1, (k6, k3tog, k6) twice, k1 (28 sts).

Row 25: Purl.

Row 26: K1, (k5, k3tog, k5) twice, k1 (24 sts).

Row 27: Purl.

Cast off.

HEAD

Using the long tail method and yarn A, cast on 8 sts.

Row 1 and foll 3 alt rows: Purl.

Row 2: (Kfb) to end (16 sts).

Row 4: (Kfb, k1) to end (24 sts).

Row 6: (Kfb, k2) to end (32 sts).

Row 8: (Kfb, k3) to end (40 sts).

Rows 9 to 21: Work 13 rows in st-st.

Row 22: (K2tog, k3) to end (32 sts).

Row 23: Purl.

Change to yarn B and dec:

Row 24: (K2tog, k2) to end (24 sts).

Row 25 and foll alt row: Purl.

Row 26: (K2tog, k1) to end (16 sts).

Row 28: (K2tog) to end (8 sts).

Break yarn and thread through sts on needle, pull tight and secure by threading yarn a second time through sts.

EYE PATCHES (make 2)

Using the long tail method and yarn C, cast on 22 sts and work in rev st-st.

Row 1: (P2tog) twice, p3, (p2tog) 4 times, p3, (p2tog) twice (14 sts).

Row 2: K2tog, k3, (k2tog) twice, k3, k2tog (10 sts).

Cast off pwise.

NOSE

Using the long tail method and yarn D, cast on 12 sts.

Break yarn and thread through sts on needle, pull tight and secure by threading yarn a second time through sts.

FEET AND LEGS (make 2)

Using the long tail method and yarn A, cast on 7 sts.

Row 1 and foll alt row: Purl.

Row 2: (Kfb) to end (14 sts).

Row 4: (Kfb, k1) to end (21 sts).

Rows 5 to 9: Work 5 rows in st-st.

Row 10: (K2tog, k1) to end (14 sts).

Rows 11 to 29: Work 19 rows in st-st.

Cast off.

HANDS AND FOREARMS (make 2)

Using the long tail method and yarn A, cast on 6 sts.

Row 1 and foll alt row: Purl.

Row 2: (Kfb) to end (12 sts).

Row 4: (Kfb, k1) to end (18 sts).

Rows 5 to 9: Work 5 rows in st-st.

Row 10: (K2tog, k1) to end (12 sts).

Rows 11 to 25: Work 15 rows in st-st.

Break yarn and thread yarn through sts and leave loose.

DUNGAREES AND STRAPS

Work dungarees and straps in yarn E, as for Monkey on page 59.

PINAFORE AND STRAPS

Work pinafore and straps in yarn F, as for Monkey on page 60.

MAKING UP

Note: Sew up all row-end seams on right side using mattress stitch one stitch in from the edge, unless otherwise stated; a one-stitch seam allowance has been allowed for this.

BODY

Sew up side edges of body and with this seam at centre back, oversew cast-on stitches. Stuff body leaving neck open.

HEAD

Sew up side edges of head leaving a gap, stuff and sew up gap. Pin and sew head to body making a horizontal stitch over one stitch from head then a horizontal stitch over one stitch from body, and do this alternately all the way round.

EYE PATCHES

Fold cast-off edge in half and oversew. Oversew row ends and pin and sew eye patches to face, sewing around outside edge.

NOSE

Oversew row ends of cast-on edge and sew nose to centre of head.

FEET AND LEGS

Gather round cast-on stitches, pull tight and secure. Sew up side edges of feet and stuff feet with tweezers or tip of scissors. Sew up side edges of legs and stuff. Pin legs to body, leaving a ¾in (2cm) gap at crotch, and sew in place.

HANDS AND FOREARMS

Gather round cast-on stitches of hands, pull tight and secure. Sew up side edges of hands and stuff hands with tweezers or tip of scissors. Sew up side edges of forearms and stuff. Pull stitches on a thread tight and secure, and sew arms to Sloth.

DUNGAREES, STRAPS AND BUTTONS

Make up dungarees, straps and buttons, as for Elephant on page 22.

PINAFORE, STRAPS AND BUTTONS

Make up pinafore, straps and buttons, as for Elephant on page 22.

FEATURES AND EMBROIDERY

Mark position of eyes with two pins and embroider eyes in black making a vertical chain stitch for each eye then a second chain stitch on top of first. Embroider mouth in stem stitch. Embroider three claws in dark brown on hands and feet (see page 155 for how to begin and fasten off invisibly for the embroidery).

MEERKAT

INFORMATION YOU'LL NEED

MATERIALS

Any DK (US: light worsted) yarn
(amounts given are approximate)
Yarn A pale brown (20g for each Meerkat) (Note: 2 separate balls of yarn A are needed)
Yarn B cream (10g)
Yarn C sapphire blue (10g)
Yarn D rain forest (15g)
Yarn E black (5g)
Yarn F dark brown (5g)
Oddment of black for embroidery
1 pair of 3.25mm (UK10:US3) needles and a spare needle of same size for dungarees
Knitters' pins and a blunt-ended needle for sewing up
Acrylic toy stuffing
2 small buttons for each Meerkat

FINISHED SIZE

Meerkat stands 8½in (21.5cm) tall

TENSION

26 sts x 34 rows measure 4in (10cm) square over st-st using 3.25mm needles and DK yarn before stuffing.

ABBREVIATIONS

See page 156

SPECIAL ABBREVIATION

w1: wrap 1 stitch – take yarn between needles to opposite side, slip 1 stitch pwise from LH needle to RH needle, then take yarn between needles to first side.

HOW TO MAKE MEERKAT

BODY

Using the long tail method and yarn A, cast on 36 sts.

Row 1: Purl.

Row 2: K1, (k8, m1, k1, m1, k8) twice, k1 (40 sts).

Rows 3 to 9: Beg with a p row, work 7 rows in st-st.

Join on yarn B and second ball of yarn A and work in intarsia, twisting yarn on WS when changing colours to avoid a hole.

Row 10: Yarn A-k13, yarn B-k14, yarn A (second ball)-k13.

Row 11: (Work in g-st to mark waist) yarn A-k13, yarn B-k14, yarn A-k13.

Row 12: Yarn A-k13, yarn B-k14, yarn A-k13.

Row 13: Yarn A-p13, yarn B-p14, yarn A-p13.

Rows 14 and 15: Rep rows 12 and 13 once.

Row 16: Yarn A-k9, k3tog, k1, yarn B-k1, k3tog, k6, k3tog, yarn A-k1, k3tog, k9, k1 (32 sts).

Row 17: Yarn A-p11, yarn B-p10, yarn A-p11.

Row 18: Yarn A-k11, yarn B-k10, yarn A-k11.

Rows 19 to 42: Rep rows 17 and 18, 12 times more, ending with a RS row.

Row 43: Yarn A-p3, (p2tog, p2) twice, yarn B-p2tog, (p2, p2tog) twice, yarn A-(p2, p2tog) twice, p3 (25 sts).

Cast off in colours as set.

HEAD

Using the long tail method and yarn A, cast on 8 sts.

Row 1 and foll 3 alt rows: Purl.

Row 2: (Kfb) to end (16 sts).

Row 4: (Kfb, k1) to end (24 sts).

Row 6: (Kfb, k2) to end (32 sts).

Row 8: (Kfb, k3) to end (40 sts).

Rows 9 to 19: Work 11 rows in st-st.

Row 20: (K2tog, k3) to end (32 sts).

Row 21 and foll 2 alt rows: Purl.

Row 22: (K2tog, k2) to end (24 sts).

Row 24: (K2tog, k1) to end (16 sts).

Row 26: (K2tog) to end (8 sts).

Break yarn and thread through sts on needle, pull tight and secure by threading yarn a second time through sts.

FEET AND LEGS (make 2)

Using the long tail method and yarn A, cast on 16 sts.

Row 1: Purl.

Row 2: (K1, kfb) 4 times, (kfb, k1) 4 times (24 sts).

Rows 3 to 9: Work 7 rows in st-st.

Row 10: K6, (k2tog) 6 times, k6 (18 sts).

Row 11: Purl.

Row 12: K7, (k2tog) twice, k7 (16 sts).

Rows 13 to 15: Work 3 rows in st-st.

Cast off.

HANDS AND FOREARMS (make 2)

Using the long tail method and yarn A, cast on 6 sts.

Row 1 and foll alt row: Purl.

Row 2: (Kfb) to end (12 sts).

Rows 3 to 21: Work 19 rows in st-st.

Row 22: (K2tog) to end (6 sts).

Break yarn, thread through sts on needle and leave loose.

DUNGAREES
(make 2 pieces)

Note: Foll individual instructions as given for 1 front and 1 back of dungarees.

First leg

Using the long tail method and yarn C, cast on 12 sts and beg in g-st.

Rows 1 and 2: Work 2 rows in g-st.

Break yarn and set aside.

Second leg

Work as for first leg but do not break yarn.

Join legs

Row 3: Beg with second leg and k10, k2tog, turn, using the knitting-on method cast on 5 sts, turn, then with the same yarn continue across first leg and k2tog, k to end (27 sts).

Row 4 and foll 2 alt rows: Purl.

Row 5: K2, m1, k23, m1, k2 (29 sts).

Row 7: K12, k2tog, k1, k2tog, k12 (27 sts).

Row 9: K10, k2tog, k3, k2tog, k10 (25 sts).

Rows 10 to 14: Work 5 rows in st-st.

Rows 15 to 17: Work 3 rows in g-st, ending with a RS row.

Cast off in g-st for back of dungarees or cont with bib for front of dungarees:

Divide for bib

Row 18: Cast off 8 sts kwise, k8 (9 sts now on RH needle), cast off rem 8 sts and fasten off.

Rejoin yarn to rem sts and patt:

****Row 19:** K2, (k1 tbl) 5 times, k2 (9 sts).

Row 20: K2, p5, k2.

Row 21: Knit.

Rows 22 to 31: Rep rows 20 and 21, 5 times more, ending with a k row.

Rows 32 and 33: Work 2 rows in g-st, ending with a RS row.

Cast off in g-st.

STRAPS FOR DUNGAREES
(make 2)

Using the long tail method and yarn C, cast on 36 sts.

Row 1: Knit.

Cast off kwise.

PINAFORE

Using the long tail method and yarn D, cast on 65 sts and beg in g-st.

Rows 1 and 2: Work 2 rows in g-st.

Rows 3 to 12: Beg with a k row, work 10 rows in st-st.

Row 13: K1, (k2tog, k2) to end (49 sts).

Rows 14 and 15: Work 2 rows in g-st, ending with a RS row.

Divide for bib

Row 16: Cast off 20 sts, k8 (9 sts now on RH needle) cast off rem 20 sts and fasten off (9 sts).

Re-join yarn to rem sts and work bib from **, as for dungarees.

STRAPS FOR PINAFORE

Make straps using yarn D, as for dungarees.

SNOUT

Using the long tail method and yarn B, cast on 20 sts.

Rows 1 to 3: Beg with a p row, work 3 rows in st-st.

Row 4: K2tog, k to the last 2 sts, k2tog (18 sts).

Row 5: Purl.

Change to yarn E and dec:

Row 6: K1, (k2tog) to last st, k1 (10 sts).

Row 7: Purl.

Break yarn and thread through sts on needle, pull tight and secure by threading yarn a second time through sts.

EYE PATCHES (make 2)

Using the long tail method and yarn F, cast on 8 sts.

Rows 1 to 4: Beg with a p row, work 4 rows in st-st, ending on a k row.

Row 5: P2, (p2tog) twice, p2 (6 sts).

Cast off.

EARS (make 2)

Using the long tail method and yarn F, cast on 11 sts.

Row 1: Purl.

Row 2: K3, (m1, k1, m1, k3) twice (15 sts).

Rows 3 and 4: Work 2 rows in st-st, ending on a k row.

Row 5: (P2tog, p1) to end (10 sts).

Break yarn and thread through sts on needle, pull tight and secure by threading yarn a second time through sts.

TAIL

Using the long tail method and yarn A, cast on 14 sts.

Row 1: Purl.

Row 2: K10, w1 (see special abbreviation), turn.

Row 3: S1p, p6, w1, turn.

Row 4: S1k, k to end.

Rows 5 to 8: Rep rows 1 to 4 once.

Rows 9 to 33: Work 25 rows in st-st.

Row 34: (K2tog) to end (7 sts).

Break yarn and thread through sts on needle, pull tight and secure by threading yarn a second time through sts.

MAKING UP

Note: Sew up all row-end seams on right side using mattress stitch one stitch in from the edge, unless otherwise stated; a one-stitch seam allowance has been allowed for this.

BODY

Sew up side edges of body and, with this seam at centre back, oversew cast-on stitches. Stuff body leaving neck open.

HEAD

Gather round cast-on stitches, pull tight and secure. Sew up side edges leaving a gap, stuff and sew up gap. Pin and sew head to body making a horizontal stitch over one stitch from head then a horizontal stitch over one stitch from body, and do this alternately all the way round.

FEET AND LEGS

Fold cast-on stitches of feet in half and oversew. Sew up side edges of legs and stuff feet and legs. Pin legs to body, leaving a ¾in (2cm) gap at crotch, and sew in place.

HANDS AND FOREARMS

Gather round cast-on stitches of forearms, pull tight and secure. Sew up side edges of forearms and stuff. Pull stitches on a thread tight and secure and sew forearms to Meerkat at both sides.

DUNGAREES, PINAFORE, STRAPS AND BUTTONS

Make up dungarees, pinafore, straps and buttons, as for Elephant on page 22.

SNOUT AND EYE PATCHES

Sew up side edges of snout and stuff. Arrange snout and eye patches on head and sew in place.

EARS

Sew up side edges of ears and press flat. Position ears and sew to head.

FEATURES

Mark position of eyes with two pins and embroider eyes in black making a vertical chain stitch for each eye, then a second chain stitch on top of first. Embroider mouth in black using straight stitches (see page 155 for how to begin and fasten off invisibly for the embroidery).

BUFFALO

INFORMATION YOU'LL NEED

MATERIALS

Any DK (US: light worsted) yarn
(amounts given are approximate)
Yarn A brown (20g)
Yarn B charcoal (5g)
Yarn C royal blue (10g)
Yarn D beige (5g)
Oddment of black for embroidery and charcoal for making up
1 pair of 3.25mm (UK10:US3) needles and a spare needle of same size for dungarees
Knitters' pins and a blunt-ended needle for sewing up
Tweezers (optional)
Acrylic toy stuffing
2 chenille stems
2 small buttons

FINISHED SIZE

Buffalo stands 7in (18cm) tall

TENSION

26 sts x 34 rows measure 4in (10cm) square over st-st using 3.25mm needles and DK yarn before stuffing.

ABBREVIATIONS

See page 156

HOW TO MAKE BUFFALO

BODY

Work body using yarn A, as for Elephant on page 18.

HEAD

Using the long tail method and yarn A, cast on 36 sts.

Row 1 and foll alt row: Purl.

Row 2: (K8, m1, k2, m1, k8) twice (40 sts).

Rows 3 to 17: Work 15 rows in st-st.

Row 18: (K2tog, k3) to end (32 sts).

Row 19 and foll 2 alt rows: Purl.

Row 20: (K2tog, k2) to end (24 sts).

Row 22: (K2tog, k1) to end (16 sts).

Row 24: (K2tog) to end (8 sts).

Break yarn and thread through sts on needle, pull tight and secure by threading yarn a second time through sts.

MUZZLE

Using the long tail method and yarn B, cast on 28 sts.

Rows 1 to 5: Beg with a p row, work 5 rows in st-st.

Row 6: *K3, (k2tog) 4 times, k3; rep from * once (20 sts).

Row 7: Purl.

Row 8: *K3, (k2tog) twice, k3; rep from * once (16 sts).

Cast off pwise.

TROTTERS AND LEGS (make 2)

Using the long tail method and yarn B, cast on 8 sts.

Row 1 and foll 2 alt rows: Purl.

Row 2: (Kfb) to end (16 sts).

Row 4: (Kfb, k1) to end (24 sts).

Row 6: (Kfb, k2) to end (32 sts).

Rows 7 to 9: Work 3 rows in st-st.

Change to yarn A and dec:

Row 10: (K2tog, k2) to end (24 sts).

Rows 11 to 21: Work 11 rows in st-st.

Cast off.

TROTTERS AND FOREARMS (make 2)

Using the long tail method and yarn B, cast on 7 sts.

Row 1 and foll alt row: Purl.

Row 2: (Kfb) to end (14 sts).

Row 4: (Kfb, k1) to end (21 sts).

Rows 5 to 9: Beg with a p row, work 5 rows in st-st.

Change to yarn A and dec:

Row 10: (K2tog, k1) to end (14 sts).

Rows 11 to 21: Work 11 rows in st-st.

Row 22: (K2tog) to end (7 sts).

Break yarn, thread through sts on needle and leave loose.

DUNGAREES AND STRAPS

Work dungarees and straps in yarn C, as for Hippo on page 28.

EARS (make 2)

Using the long tail method and yarn A, cast on 10 sts.

Row 1: Purl.

Row 2: K2, (m1, k2) to end (14 sts).

Rows 3 to 7: Work 5 rows in st-st.

Row 8: (K2tog) to end (7 sts).

Row 9: Purl.

Break yarn and thread through sts on needle, pull tight and secure by threading yarn a second time through sts.

HORNS (make 2)

Using the long tail method and yarn D, cast on 17 sts.

Rows 1 to 5: Beg with a p row, work 5 rows in st-st.

Row 6: K3, (k2tog, k2tog, k3) twice (13 sts).

Row 7: Purl.

Row 8: K2, (k2tog) twice, k1, (k2tog) twice, k2 (9 sts).

Rows 9 to 13: Beg with a p row, work 5 rows in st-st.

Row 14: K3, k3tog, k3 (7 sts).

Rows 15 to 27: Work 13 rows in st-st.

Row 28: K2, k3tog, k2 (5 sts).

Row 29: Work 3 rows in st-st.

Break yarn and thread yarn through sts on needle, pull tight and secure by threading yarn a second time through sts.

MAKING UP

Note: Sew up all row-end seams on right side using mattress stitch one stitch in from the edge, unless otherwise stated; a one-stitch seam allowance has been allowed for this.

BODY

Sew up side edges of body and, with this seam at centre back, oversew cast-on stitches. Stuff body and leave neck open.

HEAD AND MUZZLE

Sew up side edges of head and stuff leaving neck open. Sew lower edge of head to body making a horizontal stitch over one stitch from head then a horizontal stitch over one stitch from body, and do this alternately all the way round. Sew up side edges of muzzle and stuff. Pin and sew muzzle to Buffalo.

TROTTERS AND LEGS

Gather round cast-on stitches of trotters, pull tight and secure. Sew up side edges of trotters and legs and stuff. Pin legs to body, leaving a ¾in (2cm) gap at crotch, and sew in place. Shape trotters using charcoal and embroider a loop around centre of trotters and pull tight then go a second time around, and secure.

TROTTERS AND FOREARMS

Gather round cast-on stitches of trotters, pull tight and secure. Sew up side edges of trotters and forearms, stuff, and pull stitches on a thread tight and secure. Sew forearms to Buffalo at each side. Shape trotters, as for legs.

DUNGAREES, STRAPS AND BUTTONS

Make up dungarees, straps and buttons, as for Elephant on page 22.

EARS

Sew up side edges of ears and with this seam at centre back, fold cast-on stitches of ears in half and sew in place. Sew ears to Buffalo.

HORNS

Fold chenille stems in half and place fold into stitches pulled tight on a thread on wrong side. Sew up row ends of horns enclosing chenille stems inside and push a little stuffing into wide part with tweezers or tip of scissors. Cut excess chenille stems and bend horns around head with tips up. Sew horns to head of Buffalo.

FEATURES

Mark position of eyes with two pins above snout and embroider eyes in black making a vertical chain stitch for each eye then a second chain stitch on top of first. Embroider eyebrows in black using straight stitches. Embroider nostrils in black sewing long chain stitches (see page 155 for how to begin and fasten off invisibly for the embroidery).

WARTHOG

INFORMATION YOU'LL NEED

MATERIALS

Any DK (US: light worsted) yarn
(amounts given are approximate)
Yarn A ginger (20g for each Warthog)
Yarn B black (10g)
Yarn C brass (10g)
Yarn D dusky pink (15g)
Yarn E cream (5g)
Yarn F brown (5g)
Oddment of black for embroidery and for making up
1 pair of 3.25mm (UK10:US3) needles and a spare needle of same size for dungarees
Knitters' pins and a blunt-ended needle for sewing up
Acrylic toy stuffing
2 small buttons for each Warthog

FINISHED SIZE

Warthog stands 7½in (19cm) tall

TENSION

26 sts x 34 rows measure 4in (10cm) square over st-st using 3.25mm needles and DK yarn before stuffing.

ABBREVIATIONS

See page 156

HOW TO MAKE WARTHOG

BODY

Using the long tail method and yarn A, cast on 44 sts.

Row 1: Purl.

Row 2: K1, (k10, m1, k1, m1, k10) twice, k1 (48 sts).

Rows 3 to 9: Work 7 rows in st-st.

Rows 10 and 11: Work 2 rows in g-st to mark waist.

Rows 12 to 15: Beg with a k row, work 4 rows in st-st.

Row 16: K1, (k10, k3tog, k10) twice, k1 (44 sts).

Rows 17 to 19: Work 3 rows in st-st.

Row 20: K1, (k9, k3tog, k9) twice, k1 (40 sts).

Rows 21 to 23: Work 3 rows in st-st.

Row 24: K1, (k8, k3tog, k8) twice, k1 (36 sts).

Row 25: Purl.

Cast off.

HEAD

Using the long tail method and yarn A, cast on 36 sts.

Row 1: Purl.

Row 2: (K4, kfb, k4) 4 times (40 sts).

Rows 3 to 21: Work 19 rows in st-st.

Row 22: (K2tog, k3) to end (32 sts).

Row 23 and foll 2 alt rows: Purl.

Row 24: (K2tog, k2) to end (24 sts).

Row 26: (K2tog, k1) to end (16 sts).

Row 28: (K2tog) to end (8 sts).

Break yarn and thread through sts on needle, pull tight and secure by threading yarn a second time through sts.

SNOUT

Using the long tail method and yarn A, cast on 24 sts.

Rows 1 to 5: Beg with a p row, work 5 rows in st-st.

Row 6: (K3, k2tog, k2, k2tog, k3) twice (20 sts).

Rows 7 to 9: Work 3 rows in st-st.

Row 10: (K2, k2tog, k2, k2tog, k2) twice (16 sts).

Rows 11 to 13: Work 3 rows in st-st.

Row 14: (K1, k2tog, k2, k2tog, k1) twice (12 sts).

Rows 15 to 17: K 1 row then p 2 rows.

Row 18: (K2tog) to end (6 sts).

Break yarn and thread through sts on needle, pull tight and secure by threading yarn a second time through sts.

TROTTERS AND LEGS (make 2)

Using the long tail method and yarn B, cast on 7 sts.

Row 1 and foll alt row: Purl.

Row 2: (Kfb) to end (14 sts).

Row 4: (Kfb, k1) to end (21 sts).

Rows 5 to 9: Work 5 rows in st-st.

Change to yarn A and dec:

Row 10: (K2tog, k1) to end (14 sts).

Rows 11 to 21: Work 11 rows in st-st.

Cast off.

TROTTERS AND FOREARMS (make 2)

Using the long tail method and yarn B, cast on 8 sts.

Row 1: Purl.

Row 2: (Kfb) to end (16 sts).

Rows 3 to 7: Work 5 rows in st-st.

Change to yarn A and dec:

Row 8: (K2tog, k2) to end (12 sts).

Rows 9 to 21: Work 13 rows in st-st.

Row 22: (K2tog, k1) to end (8 sts).

Break yarn, thread through sts on needle and leave loose.

DUNGAREES
(make 2 pieces)

Note: Foll individual instructions as given for 1 front and 1 back of dungarees.

First leg

Using the long tail method and yarn C, cast on 12 sts and beg in g-st.

Rows 1 and 2: Work 2 rows in g-st.

Break yarn and set aside.

Second leg

Work as for first leg but do not break yarn.

Join legs

Row 3: Beg with second leg and k10, k2tog, turn, using the knitting-on method cast on 5 sts, turn, then with the same yarn continue across first leg and k2tog, k to end (27 sts).

Row 4 and foll 2 alt rows: Purl.

Row 5: (K2, m1) twice, k19, (m1, k2) twice (31 sts).

Row 7: (K2, m1) twice, k9, k2tog, k1, k2tog, k9, (m1, k2) twice (33 sts).

Row 9: K13, k2tog, k3, k2tog, k13 (31 sts).

Rows 10 to 14: Work 5 rows in st-st.

Rows 15 to 17: Work 3 rows in g-st, ending with a RS row.

Cast off in g-st for back of dungarees or cont with bib for front of dungarees:

Divide for bib

Row 18: Cast off 9 sts kwise, k12 (13 sts now on RH needle), cast off rem 9 sts and fasten off.

Re-join yarn to rem sts and patt:

****Row 19:** K2, (k1 tbl) 9 times, k2 (13 sts).

Row 20: K2, p9, k2.

Row 21: Knit.

Rows 22 to 27: Rep rows 20 and 21, 3 times more, ending with a k row.

Rows 28 and 29: Work 2 rows in g-st, ending with a RS row.

Cast off in g-st.

STRAPS FOR DUNGAREES
(make 2)

Using the long tail method and yarn C, cast on 30 sts.

Row 1: Knit.

Cast off kwise.

PINAFORE

Using the long tail method and yarn D, cast on 81 sts and beg in g-st.

Rows 1 and 2: Work 2 rows in g-st.

Rows 3 to 14: Beg with a k row, work 12 rows in st-st.

Row 15: K1, (k2tog, k2) to end (61 sts).

Rows 16 and 17: Work 2 rows in g-st, ending with a RS row.

Divide for bib

Row 18: Cast off 24 sts kwise, k12 (13 sts now on RH needle) cast off rem 24 sts and fasten off.

Re-join yarn to rem sts and work bib from **, as for dungarees.

STRAPS FOR PINAFORE
(make 2)

Using yarn D make straps, as for dungarees.

EARS (make 2)

Using the long tail method and yarn A, cast on 12 sts.

Rows 1 to 3: Beg with a p row, work 3 rows in st-st.

Row 4: K1, m1, k to last st, m1, k1 (14 sts).

Rows 5 to 7: Work 3 rows in st-st.

Row 8: K2tog, (k1, k2tog) to end (9 sts).

Row 9: Purl.

Row 10: K2tog, k to last 2 sts, k2tog (7 sts).

Break yarn and thread through sts on needle, pull tight and secure by threading yarn a second time through sts.

WARTS (make 2)
Using the long tail method and yarn A, cast on 10 sts.
Rows 1 to 3: Beg with a p row, work 3 rows in st-st.
Row 4: K1, (k2tog, k1) to end (7 sts).
Break yarn and thread through sts on needle, pull tight and secure by threading yarn a second time through sts.

BASE OF TUSKS (make 2)
Using the long tail method and yarn A, cast on 12 sts.
Rows 1 to 4: P 1 row then k 3 rows.
Row 5: (P2tog) to end (6 sts).
Break yarn and thread through sts on needle, pull tight and secure by threading yarn a second time through sts.

TUSKS FOR BOAR AND SOW (make 2)
Using the long tail method and yarn E, cast on 9 sts.
Rows 1 to 5: Beg with a p row, work 5 rows in st-st.
Row 6: (K2tog, k1) to end (6 sts).
Break yarn and thread through sts on needle, pull tight and secure by threading yarn a second time through sts.

TUSKS FOR BOAR (make 2)
Using the long tail method and yarn E, cast on 12 sts.
Rows 1 to 9: Beg with a p row, work 9 rows in st-st.
Row 10: (K2tog, k1) to end (8 sts).
Break yarn and thread through sts on needle, pull tight and secure by threading yarn a second time through sts.

MANE

Using the long tail method and yarn F, cast on 20 sts loosely and work loop-st and at the same time cast off:

Row 1: K1, *knit next st, placing index finger of LH behind RH needle and wind yarn round finger and needle clockwise twice, then wind just round needle in the same direction once. Knit st pulling 3 loops through, place these loops on LH needle and k into the back of them, pass first st on RH needle over second and off the needle. Pull on loops just made to secure (this will be referred to as loop-st), rep from * to last st, k1 (2 sts).

Pass first st over second and off the needle, and fasten off.

TAIL

Using the long tail method and yarn A, cast on 15 sts.

Cast off kwise.

MAKING UP

Note: Sew up all row-end seams on right side using mattress stitch one stitch in from the edge, unless otherwise stated; a one-stitch seam allowance has been allowed for this.

BODY

Sew up side edges of body and with this seam at centre back, oversew cast-on stitches. Stuff body and leave neck open.

HEAD AND SNOUT

Sew up side edges of head and stuff leaving neck open. Sew lower edge of head to body, making a horizontal stitch over one stitch from head then a horizontal stitch over one stitch from body, and do this alternately all the way round. Sew up side edges of snout and stuff. Pin and sew snout to Warthog.

TROTTERS AND LEGS

Gather round cast-on stitches of trotters, pull tight and secure. Sew up side edges of trotters and legs and stuff. Pin legs to body, leaving a ¾in (2cm) gap at crotch, and sew in place. Shape trotters using black and embroider a loop around centre of trotters, pull tight, then go a second time around and secure.

TROTTERS AND FOREARMS

Gather round cast-on stitches of trotters, pull tight and secure. Sew up side edges of trotters and forearms, stuff, and pull stitches on a thread tight and secure. Sew forearms to Warthog at each side. Shape trotters, as for legs.

DUNGAREES, PINAFORE, STRAPS AND BUTTONS

Make up dungarees, straps and buttons, as for Elephant on page 22.

EARS

Sew up side edges of ears and press flat. Pin and sew ears to head.

FEATURES

Mark position of eyes with two pins above snout and embroider eyes in black making a vertical chain stitch for each eye, then a second chain stitch on top of first. Embroider eyebrows in black using straight stitches (see page 155 for how to begin and fasten off invisibly for the embroidery).

WARTS

Sew row ends of warts together and place a tiny amount of stuffing inside. Sew warts to snout.

BASE OF TUSKS, TUSKS AND TUSKS FOR BOAR

Sew up row ends of base of tusks and stuff. Sew to each side of snout. Roll up tusks from row ends to row ends and sew in place. Sew one tusk to each side of base for sow, and sew two tusks to each side of base for boar.

MANE

Fold mane in half and oversew. Sew mane to head.

TAIL

Fold over tip of tail and sew in place. Position tail at rear of Warthog below waistband and sew in place.

GORILLA

INFORMATION YOU'LL NEED

MATERIALS

Any DK (US: light worsted) yarn
(amounts given are approximate)
Yarn A charcoal (20g)
Yarn B dark grey (5g)
Yarn C petrol blue (10g)
Oddment of black for embroidery
1 pair of 3.25mm (UK10:US3) needles
Knitters' pins and a blunt-ended needle for sewing up
Tweezers (optional)
Acrylic toy stuffing
2 small buttons

FINISHED SIZE

Gorilla measures 6½in (16.5cm) high

TENSION

26 sts x 34 rows measure 4in (10cm) square over st-st using 3.25mm needles and DK yarn before stuffing.

ABBREVIATIONS

See page 156

SPECIAL ABBREVIATION

w1: wrap 1 stitch – take yarn between needles to opposite side, slip 1 stitch pwise from LH needle to RH needle, then take yarn between needles to first side.

HOW TO MAKE GORILLA

BODY

Using the long tail method and yarn A, cast on 32 sts.

Row 1: Purl.

Row 2: K7, (m1, k1) 4 times, k11, (m1, k1) 4 times, k6 (40 sts).

Rows 3 to 17: Work 15 rows in st-st.

Rows 18 and 19: Work 2 rows in g-st for waist.

Rows 20 to 29: Beg with a k row, work 10 rows in st-st.

Row 30: K1, (k8, k3tog, k8) twice, k1, (36 sts).

Row 31: Purl.

Row 32: K1, (k7, k3tog, k7) twice, k1, (32 sts).

Row 33: Purl.

Cast off.

HEAD

Using the long tail method and yarn A, cast on 32 sts.

Row 1: Purl.

Row 2: (Kfb, k1) to end (48 sts).

Rows 3 to 15: Work 13 rows in st-st.

Row 16: (K2tog, k4) to end (40 sts).

Row 17 and foll 3 alt rows: Purl.

Row 18: (K2tog, k3) to end (32 sts).

Row 20: (K2tog, k2) to end (24 sts).

Row 22: (K2tog, k1) to end (16 sts).

Row 24: (K2tog) to end (8 sts).

Break yarn and thread through sts on needle, pull tight and secure by threading yarn a second time through sts.

MUZZLE

Using the long tail method and yarn B, cast on 20 sts.

Row 1: Purl.

Row 2: K1, (m1, k2) to last st, m1, k1 (30 sts).

Rows 3 to 9: Work 7 rows in st-st.

Row 10: K4, (k2tog) 4 times, k6, (k2tog) 4 times, k4 (22 sts).

Row 11: Purl.

Row 12: K2, (k2tog) 4 times, k2, (k2tog) 4 times, k2 (14 sts).

Row 13: Purl.

Break yarn and thread through sts on needle, pull tight and secure by threading yarn a second time through sts.

FACE PIECE

Using the long tail method and yarn B, cast on 8 sts.

Row 1: Purl.

Row 2: K1, (m1, k1) to end (15 sts).

Rows 3 to 7: Work 5 rows in st-st.

Row 8: (K2tog) twice, k7, (k2tog) twice (11 sts).

Row 9: Purl.

Row 10: (K2tog) twice, k3, (k2tog) twice (7 sts).

Row 11: Purl.

Break yarn and thread through sts on needle, pull tight and secure by threading yarn a second time through sts.

NOSE

Using the long tail method and yarn B, cast on 6 sts.

Rows 1 to 4: Beg with a p row, work 4 rows in st-st, ending with a k row.

Break yarn and thread through sts on needle, pull tight and secure by threading yarn a second time through sts.

DUNGAREES

Using the long tail method and yarn C, cast on 32 sts.

Row 1 and foll 2 alt rows: Purl.

Row 2: K5, (m1, k2) 4 times, k8, (m1, k2) 4 times, k3 (40 sts).

Row 4: K7, (m1, k2) 4 times, k12, (m1, k2) 4 times, k5 (48 sts).

Row 6: K9, (m1, k2) 4 times, k16, (m1, k2) 4 times, k7 (56 sts).

Rows 7 to 19: Work 13 rows in st-st.
Rows 20 to 22: Work 3 rows in g-st, ending with a RS row.
Divide for bib
Row 23: Cast off 21 sts kwise, k13 (14 sts now on RH needle), cast off rem 21 sts kwise and fasten off.
Re-join yarn to rem sts and patt:
Row 24: K2, (k1 tbl) 10 times, k2 (14 sts).
Row 25: K2, p10, k2.
Row 26: Knit.
Rows 27 to 30: Rep rows 25 and 26 twice more, ending with a k row.
Rows 31 and 32: Work 2 rows in g-st, ending with a RS row.
Cast off in g-st.

LEGS (make 2)

Using the long tail method and yarn C, cast on 10 sts.
Row 1: Purl.
Row 2: (Kfb) to end (20 sts).
Rows 3 to 7: Work 5 rows in st-st.
Row 8: K16, w1 (see special abbreviation), turn.
Row 9: S1p, p12, w1, turn.
Row 10: S1k, k to end.
Row 11: Purl.
Rows 12 to 15: Work 4 rows in g-st.
Rows 16 and 17: Change to yarn A and k 1 row then p 1 row.
Rows 18 to 29: Rep rows 8 to 11, 3 times more.
Row 30: (K2tog, k2) to end (15 sts).
Row 31: Purl.
Row 32: (K2tog, k1) to end (10 sts).
Break yarn and thread through sts on needle, pull tight and secure by threading yarn a second time through sts.

FEET (make 2)

Using the long tail method and yarn B, cast on 8 sts.
Row 1: Purl.
Row 2: (Kfb) to end (16 sts).
Rows 3 to 7: Work 5 rows in st-st.
Row 8: K6, m1, k4, m1, k6 (18 sts).
Row 9: Purl.
Row 10: K6, cast off 6 sts (7 sts now on RH needle), k to end (12 sts).
Rows 11 to 13: Push rem sts together and work 3 rows in st-st.
Row 14: (K2tog) to end (6 sts).
Break yarn and thread through sts on needle, pull tight and secure by threading yarn a second time through sts.

HANDS AND FOREARMS (make 2)

Using the long tail method and yarn A, cast on 9 sts.
Row 1: Purl.
Row 2: (Kfb) to end (18 sts).
Rows 3 to 7: Work 5 rows in st-st.
Row 8: K13, w1 (see special abbreviation), turn.
Row 9: S1p, p8, w1, turn.
Row 10: S1k, k to end.
Rows 11 to 13: Work 3 rows in st-st.
Rows 14 to 31: Rep rows 8 to 13, 3 times more.
Rows 32 to 37: Change to yarn B and work 6 rows in st-st.
Row 38: K6, cast off 6 sts (7 sts now on RH needle), k to end (12 sts).
Rows 39 to 41: Push rem sts together and work 3 rows in st-st.
Row 42: (K2tog) to end (6 sts).
Break yarn and thread through sts on needle, pull tight and secure by threading yarn a second time through sts.

STRAPS FOR DUNGAREES (make 2)

Using the long tail method and yarn C, cast on 26 sts.
Row 1: Knit.
Cast off kwise.

MAKING UP

Note: Sew up all row-end seams on right side using mattress stitch one stitch in from the edge, unless otherwise stated; a one-stitch seam allowance has been allowed for this.

BODY

Sew up side edges of body and with this seam at centre back, oversew cast-on stitches. Stuff body leaving neck open.

HEAD

Sew up side edges of head and stuff leaving neck open. Pin and sew head to body making a horizontal stitch over one stitch from head then a horizontal stitch over one stitch from body, and do this alternately all the way round.

MUZZLE AND FACE PIECE

Sew up side edges of muzzle and with this seam at centre of underneath, sew across cast-off stitches. Stuff muzzle and arrange muzzle and face piece on face and pin and sew in place.

NOSE

Sew outside edge of nose to top of muzzle leaving a gap, stuff with tweezers or tip of scissors and sew up gap.

DUNGAREES

Sew up side edges of dungarees and with this seam at centre of back, sew across cast-on stitches. Place dungarees on Gorilla and sew cast-off stitches of dungarees to row above waist using back stitch all the way round.

LEGS AND FEET

Gather round cast-on stitches of legs, pull tight and secure. Sew up side edges of legs leaving a gap, stuff and sew up gap. Assemble Gorilla on a flat surface and pin and sew legs to sides of body. Fold cast-off stitches of big toe in half, sew up and fasten off. Sew up side edges of feet and stuff feet and big toe with tweezers or tip of scissors. Fold cast-on stitches in half and oversew. Pin and sew feet to legs.

HANDS AND FOREARMS

Fold cast-off stitches of thumb in half, sew up and fasten off. Sew up side edges of hand and place a small ball of stuffing into hands and stuff thumb with tweezers or tip of scissors. Gather round cast-on stitches, pull tight and secure. Sew up side edges of forearms and stuff as you sew. Sew forearms to body of Gorilla at each side.

STRAPS FOR DUNGAREES AND BUTTONS

Sew ends of straps to bib, take straps over shoulders, cross over and sew to back waist. Add two buttons to bib.

FEATURES

Mark position of eyes with two pins and embroider eyes in black making a vertical chain stitch for each eye, then a second chain stitch on top of first. Embroider nostrils in black using straight stitches (see page 155 for how to begin and fasten off invisibly for the embroidery).

PORCUPINE

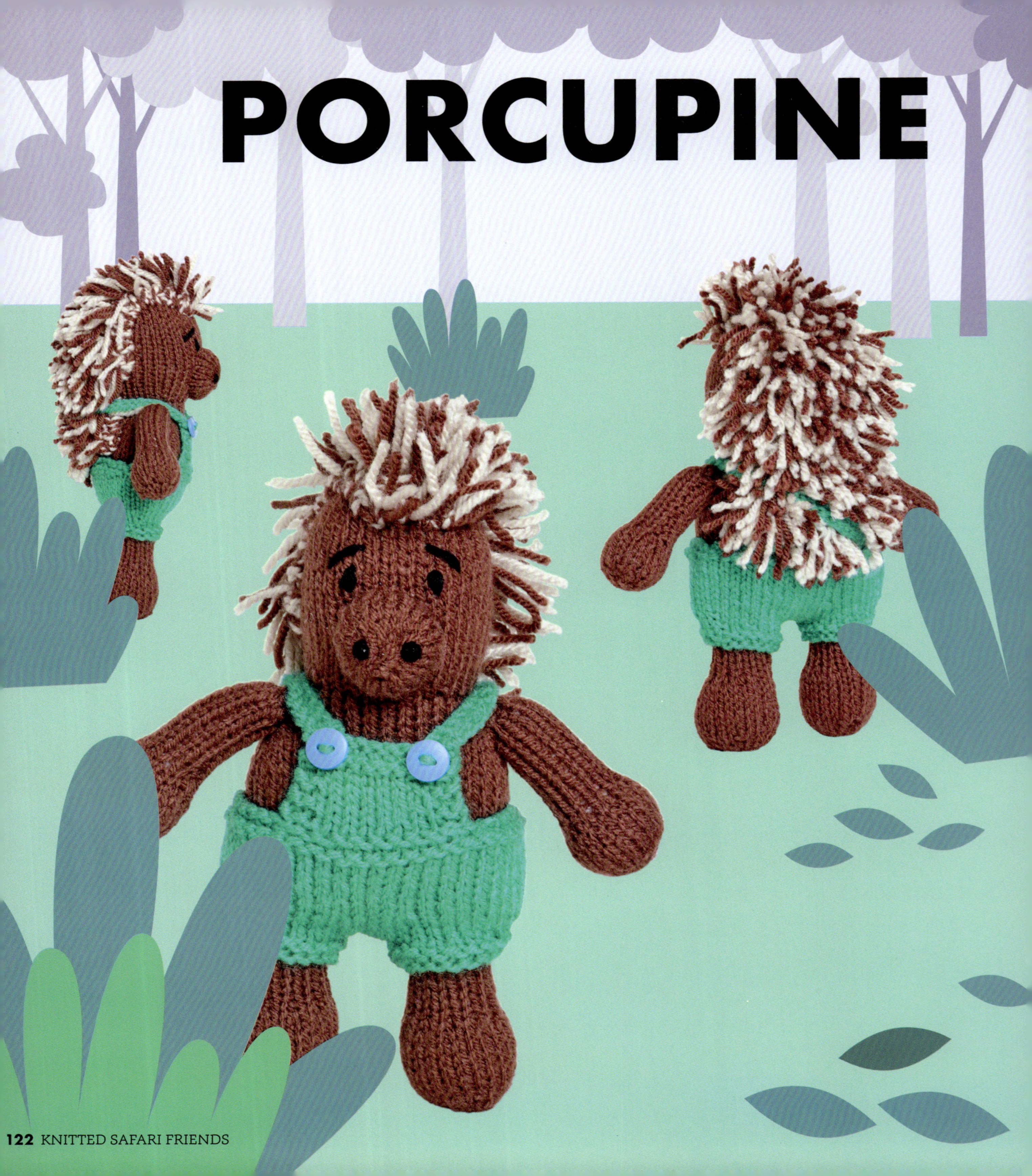

INFORMATION YOU'LL NEED

MATERIALS

Any DK (US: light worsted) yarn (amounts given are approximate)
Yarn A brown (15g)
Yarn B emerald green (10g)
Yarn C beige (10g)
Oddment of black for embroidery
1 pair of 3.25mm (UK10:US3) needles and a spare needle of same size for dungarees
Knitters' pins and a blunt-ended needle for sewing up
Acrylic toy stuffing
2 small buttons

FINISHED SIZE

Porcupine stands 7½in (9cm) tall

TENSION

26 sts x 34 rows measure 4in (10cm) square over st-st using 3.25mm needles and DK yarn before stuffing.

ABBREVIATIONS

See page 156

HOW TO MAKE PORCUPINE

BODY

Using the long tail method and yarn A, cast on 36 sts.

Row 1: Purl.

Row 2: K1, (k8, m1, k1, m1, k8) twice, k1 (40 sts).

Rows 3 to 9: Beg with a p row, work 7 rows in st-st.

Rows 10 and 11: Work 2 rows in g-st to mark waist.

Rows 12 to 17: Work 6 rows in st-st.

Row 18: K1, (k8, k3tog, k8) twice, k1 (36 sts).

Row 19 and foll alt row: Purl.

Row 20: K1, (k7, k3tog, k7) twice, k1 (32 sts).

Row 22: K1, (k6, k3tog, k6) twice, k1 (28 sts).

Row 23: Purl.

Cast off.

HEAD

Using the long tail method and yarn A, cast on 28 sts.

Row 1: Purl.

Row 2: K8, (m1, k4) 4 times, k4 (32 sts).

Rows 3 to 19: Work 17 rows in st-st.

Row 20: (K2tog, k2) to end (24 sts).

Row 21 and foll alt row: Purl.

Row 22: (K2tog, k1) to end (16 sts).

Row 24: (K2tog) to end (8 sts).

Break yarn and thread through sts on needle, pull tight and secure by threading yarn a second time through sts.

FEET AND LEGS (make 2)

Using the long tail method and yarn A, cast on 16 sts.

Row 1: Purl.

Row 2: (K1, kfb) 4 times, (kfb, k1) 4 times (24 sts).

Rows 3 to 9: Work 7 rows in st-st.

Row 10: K2, (k2tog) 10 times, k2 (14 sts).

Rows 11 to 19: Work 9 rows in st-st.

Cast off.

HANDS AND FOREARMS (make 2)

Using the long tail method and yarn A, cast on 10 sts.

Row 1: Purl.

Row 2: (Kfb) to end (20 sts).

Rows 3 to 7: Work 5 rows in st-st.

Row 8: (K2tog) to end (10 sts).

Rows 9 to 21: Work 13 rows in st-st.

Row 22: K1, (k2tog, k1) to end (7 sts).

Break yarn, thread through sts on needle and leave loose.

DUNGAREES (make 2 pieces)

First leg

Using the long tail method and yarn B, cast on 10 sts and beg in g-st.

Rows 1 and 2: Work 2 rows in g-st.

Break yarn and set aside.

Second leg

Work as for first leg but do not break yarn.

Join legs

Row 3: Beg with second leg and k8, k2tog, turn, using the knitting-on method cast on 5 sts, turn, then with the same yarn continue across first leg and k2tog, k to end (23 sts).

Row 4 and foll 2 alt rows: Purl.

Row 5: (K2, m1) twice, k15, (m1, k2) twice (27 sts).

Row 7: K2, m1, k9, k2tog, k1, k2tog, k9, m1, k2 (27 sts).

Row 9: K10, k2tog, k3, k2tog, k10 (25 sts).

Rows 10 to 14: Work 5 rows in st-st.
Rows 15 to 17: Work 3 rows in g-st, ending with a RS row.
Cast off in g-st for back of dungarees or cont with bib for front of dungarees:
Divide for bib
Row 18: Cast off 7 sts kwise, k10 (11 sts now on RH needle), cast off rem 7 sts and fasten off.
Rejoin yarn to rem sts and patt:
Row 19: K2, (k1 tbl) 7 times, k2 (11 sts).
Row 20: K2, p7, k2.
Row 21: Knit.
Rows 22 to 25: Rep rows 20 and 21 twice more, ending with a k row.
Rows 26 and 27: Work 2 rows in g-st, ending with a RS row.
Cast off in g-st.

SNOUT

Using the long tail method and yarn A, cast on 18 sts.
Row 1: Purl.
Row 2: K3, (m1, k3) to end (23 sts).
Rows 3 to 5: Work 3 rows in st-st.
Row 6: K2tog, (k1, k2tog) to end (15 sts).
Row 7: Purl.
Break yarn and thread through sts on needle, pull tight and secure by threading yarn a second time through sts.

SPINES

Note: Use yarn A and yarn C held together treated as one strand throughout.
Using the long tail method and yarn A and C, cast on 12 sts loosely.
Row 1: K1, *k next st placing index finger of LH behind RH needle and wind yarn round finger and needle clockwise once, then wind just round needle in the same direction once, k st pulling 2 loops through, place these loops on LH needle and k into the back of them, pull on loop just made to secure (this will be referred to as loop-st); rep from * 10 times more, k1.
Row 2: Knit.
Row 3 and foll 17 alt rows: K1, (loop-st) to last st, k1.
Row 4: K1, k2tog, k to last 3 sts, k2tog, k1 (10 sts).
Row 6: Knit.
Row 8: As row 4 (8 sts).
Row 10: Knit.
Row 12: K1, kfb, k to last 2 sts, kfb, k1 (10 sts).
Row 14: As row 12 (12 sts).
Row 16: Knit.
Row 18: Knit.
Row 20: Knit.
Row 22: K1, k2tog, k to last 3 sts, k2tog, k1 (10 sts).
Row 24: Knit.
Row 26: As row 22 (8 sts).
Row 28: Knit.
Row 30: As row 22 (6 sts).
Row 32: Knit.
Row 34: Knit.
Row 36: Knit.
Row 38: K2tog, k2, k2tog (4 sts).
Cast off kwise.

STRAPS (make 2)

Using the long tail method and yarn B, cast on 26 sts.
Row 1: Knit.
Cast off kwise.

MAKING UP

Note: Sew up all row-end seams on right side using mattress stitch one stitch in from the edge, unless otherwise stated; a one-stitch seam allowance has been allowed for this.

BODY

Sew up side edges of body and with this seam at centre back, oversew cast-on stitches. Stuff body leaving neck open.

HEAD

Sew up side edges of head and stuff. Pin and sew head to body by making a horizontal stitch over one stitch from head, then a horizontal stitch over one stitch from body and do this alternately all the way round.

FEET AND LEGS

Fold cast-on stitches of feet in half and oversew. Sew up side edges of legs and stuff feet and legs. Pin legs to body, leaving a ¾in (2cm) gap at crotch, and sew in place.

HANDS AND FOREARMS

Gather round cast-on stitches of forearms, pull tight and secure. Sew up side edges of forearms and stuff. Pull stitches on a thread tight and secure. Sew forearms to Porcupine at both sides.

DUNGAREES

Place two pieces of dungarees together matching all edges and sew up inside leg seams and across crotch. Sew up side seams and place dungarees on Porcupine. Sew cast-off stitches of waist of dungarees to row above waist of Porcupine using back stitch all the way round.

SNOUT

Sew up side edges of snout and stuff. Pin and sew snout to head.

SPINES

Sew cast-on stitches of spines to waist of Porcupine at back. Then sew around all edges, folding cast-off stitches under at forehead. Cut through all loops.

STRAPS AND BUTTONS

Sew ends of straps to top edge of front of bib, take straps over shoulders, cross over and sew to back of dungarees. Add two buttons to bib.

FEATURES

Mark position of eyes with two pins and embroider eyes in black making a vertical chain stitch for each eye, then a second chain stitch on top of first. Embroider eyebrows in black using straight stitches and embroider nostrils using chain stitches on snout (see page 155 for how to begin and fasten off invisibly for the embroidery).

ANTELOPE

INFORMATION YOU'LL NEED

MATERIALS

Any DK (US: light worsted) yarn
(amounts given are approximate)
Yarn A pale brown (15g)
Yarn B white (5g)
Yarn C green (10g)
Yarn D golden cream (5g)
Yarn E black (2g)
Oddment of black for embroidery and white for making up
1 pair of 3.25mm (UK10:US3) needles and a spare needle of same size for dungarees
Knitters' pins and a blunt-ended needle for sewing up
Acrylic toy stuffing
2 small buttons
4 chenille stems

FINISHED SIZE

Antelope stands 10½in (26.5cm) tall

TENSION

26 sts x 34 rows measure 4in (10cm) square over st-st using 3.25mm needles and DK yarn before stuffing.

ABBREVIATIONS

See page 156

HOW TO MAKE ANTELOPE

BODY

Using the long tail method and yarn A, cast on 32 sts.

Row 1: Purl.

Row 2: K1, (k7, m1, k1, m1, k7) twice, k1 (36 sts).

Rows 3 to 9: Work 7 rows in st-st.

Rows 10 and 11: Work 2 rows in g-st to mark waist.

Rows 12 to 21: Beg with a k row, work 10 rows in st-st.

Row 22: K1, (k7, k3tog, k7) twice, k1 (32 sts).

Row 23 and foll alt row: Purl.

Row 24: K1, (k6, k3tog, k6) twice, k1 (28 sts).

Row 26: K1, (k5, k3tog, k5) twice, k1 (24 sts).

Row 27: Purl.

Cast off.

HEAD

Note: Before beg, cut 2 lengths of yarn B 40in (100cm) long and reserve.

Using the long tail method and yarn A, cast on 24 sts.

Row 1 and foll alt row: Purl.

Row 2: (Kfb, k2) to end (32 sts).

Row 4: (Kfb, k3) to end (40 sts).

Row 5: Purl.

Join on reserved pieces of yarn B and work in yarn A and B, carrying yarn A loosely behind yarn B and twisting yarn when changing colours to avoid a hole.

Row 6: Yarn A-k16, yarn B-(first piece) k2, yarn A-k4, yarn B-(second piece) k2, yarn A-k16.

Row 7: Yarn A-p16, yarn B-p2, yarn A-p4, yarn B-p2, yarn A-p16.

Row 8: Yarn A-k16, yarn B-k2, yarn A-k4, yarn B-k2, yarn A-k16.

Row 9: As row 7.

Rows 10 to 13: Rep rows 8 and 9 twice more.

Row 14: Yarn A-k12, k2tog, k2, yarn B-k2, yarn A-k1, m1, k2, m1, k1, yarn B-k2, yarn A-k2, k2tog, k12 (40 sts).

Row 15: Yarn A-p15, yarn B-p2, yarn A-p6, yarn B-p2, yarn A-p15.

Row 16: Yarn A-k15, yarn B-k2, yarn A-k6, yarn B-k2, yarn A-k15.

Row 17: As row 15.

Row 18: Yarn A-k12, k2tog, k1, yarn B-k2, yarn A-k2, (m1, k2) twice, yarn B-k2, yarn A-k1, k2tog, k12 (40 sts).

Row 19: Yarn A-p14, yarn B-p2, yarn A-p8, yarn B-p2, yarn A-p14.

Row 20: Yarn A-k2, (k2tog, k2) 3 times, yarn B-k2, yarn A-k8, yarn B-k2, yarn A-k2, (k2tog, k2) 3 times (34 sts).

Row 21: Yarn A-p2tog, (p1, p2tog) 3 times, yarn B-p2, yarn A-p8, yarn B-p2, yarn A-p2tog, (p1, p2tog) 3 times (26 sts).

Cast off in yarn A.

SNOUT

Using the long tail method and yarn B, cast on 21 sts.

Rows 1 to 5: Beg with a p row, work 5 rows in st-st.

Row 6: (K2tog, k1) to end (14 sts).

Row 7: Purl.

Row 8: (K2tog) to end (7 sts).

Break yarn and thread through sts on needle, pull tight and secure by threading yarn a second time through sts.

TROTTERS AND LEGS (make 2)

Using the long tail method and yarn B, cast on 8 sts.

Row 1 and foll alt row: Purl.

Row 2: (Kfb) to end (16 sts).

Row 4: (Kfb, k1) to end (24 sts).

Rows 5 to 9: Work 5 rows in st-st.

Change to yarn A and dec:

Row 10: (K2tog, k1) to end (16 sts).

Rows 11 to 25: Work 15 rows in st-st.

Cast off.

TROTTERS AND FOREARMS (make 2)

Using the long tail method and yarn B, cast on 8 sts.

Row 1: Purl.

Row 2: (Kfb) to end (16 sts).

Rows 3 to 7: Work 5 rows in st-st.
Change to yarn A and dec:
Row 8: K2, k2tog, (k3, k2tog) twice, k2 (13 sts).
Rows 9 to 25: Work 17 rows in st-st.
Row 26: K1, (k2tog, k1) to end (9 sts).
Break yarn, thread through sts on needle and leave loose.

DUNGAREES (make 2 pieces)

Note: Foll individual instructions as given for 1 front and 1 back of dungarees.

First leg
Using the long tail method and yarn C, cast on 12 sts and beg in g-st.
Rows 1 and 2: Work 2 rows in g-st.
Break yarn and set aside.

Second leg
Work as for first leg but do not break yarn.

Join legs
Row 3: Beg with second leg and k10, k2tog, turn, using the knitting-on method cast on 5 sts, turn, then with the same yarn continue across first leg and k2tog, k to end (27 sts).
Rows 4 to 6: Beg with a p row, work 3 rows in st-st.
Row 7: K11, k2tog, k1, k2tog, k11 (25 sts).
Row 8: Purl.
Row 9: K9, k2tog, k3, k2tog, k9 (23 sts).
Rows 10 to 14: Work 5 rows in st-st.
Rows 15 to 17: Work 3 rows in g-st, ending with a RS row.
Cast off in g-st for back of dungarees or cont with bib for front of dungarees:

Divide for bib
Row 18: Cast off 6 sts kwise, k10 (11 sts now on RH needle), cast off rem 6 sts and fasten off.
Rejoin yarn to rem sts and patt:
Row 19: K2, (k1 tbl) 7 times, k2 (11 sts).
Row 20: K2, p7, k2.
Row 21: Knit.
Rows 22 to 27: Rep rows 20 and 21, 3 times more, ending with a k row.
Rows 28 and 29: Work 2 rows in g-st, ending with a RS row.
Cast off in g-st.

STRAPS FOR DUNGAREES (make 2)

Using the long tail method and yarn C, cast on 26 sts.
Row 1: Knit.
Cast off kwise.

ANTLERS (make 2)

Using the long tail method and yarn D, cast on 11 sts and work in g-st.
Rows 1 to 10: Work 10 rows in g-st.
Row 11: K1, k2tog, k5, k2tog, k1 (9 sts).
Rows 12 to 26: Work 15 rows in g-st.
Row 27: K1, k2tog, k3, k2tog, k1 (7 sts).
Rows 28 to 42: Work 15 rows in g-st.
Break yarn and thread through sts on needle, pull tight and secure by threading yarn a second time through sts.

EARS (make 2)

Using the long tail method and yarn A, cast on 10 sts.
Row 1: Purl.
Row 2: K2, (m1, k2) to end (14 sts).
Rows 3 to 7: Work 5 rows in st-st.
Change to yarn E and dec:
Row 8: (K2tog) to end (7 sts).
Rows 9 to 11: Work 3 rows in st-st.
Break yarn and thread through sts on needle, pull tight and secure by threading yarn a second time through sts.

MAKING UP

Note: Sew up all row-end seams on right side using mattress stitch one stitch in from the edge, unless otherwise stated; a one-stitch seam allowance has been allowed for this.

BODY

Sew up side edges of body and with this seam at centre back, oversew cast-on stitches. Stuff body leaving neck open.

HEAD AND SNOUT

Weave in ends around colour work. Sew up side edges of head and with seam at centre of back, sew across cast-off stitches. Pin head to body and sew in place making a short horizontal stitch over one stitch from head, and a short horizontal stitch over one stitch from body and do this alternately all the way round. Sew up side edges of snout and stuff. Pin and sew snout to front of head.

TROTTERS AND LEGS

Gather round cast-on stitches of trotters, pull tight and secure. Sew up side edges of trotters and legs, stuff trotters then stuff legs. Pin legs to body, leaving a ¾in (2cm) gap at crotch, and sew in place. Shape trotters using white and embroider a loop around centre of trotters, pull tight, then go a second time around and secure.

TROTTERS AND FOREARMS

Gather round cast-on stitches of trotters, pull tight and secure. Sew up side edges of trotters and forearms, stuff trotters then stuff forearms. Pull stitches on a thread tight and secure. Sew forearms to Antelope at each side. Shape trotters in white, as for legs.

DUNGAREES, STRAPS AND BUTTONS

Make up dungarees, straps and buttons, as for Elephant on page 22.

ANTLERS

Place two chenille stems together and fold in half and place fold on wrong side of stitches pulled tight on a thread and sew up side edges of antlers enclosing chenille stems inside. Push a little stuffing inside wide part with tweezers or tip of scissors. Twist antlers around a pencil to shape and sew to top of head.

EARS

Oversew side edges of ears and with this seam at centre back, fold cast-on stitches of ears in half and sew in place. Position ears and pin and sew ears to Antelope.

FEATURES

Mark position of eyes with two pins and embroider eyes in black making a vertical chain stitch for each eye, then a second chain stitch on top of first. Embroider nose in black using satin stitch and a straight stitch (see page 155 for how to begin and fasten off invisibly for the embroidery).

CROCODILE

INFORMATION YOU'LL NEED

MATERIALS

Any DK (US: light worsted) yarn (amounts given are approximate)
Yarn A green (20g)
Yarn B tangerine (10g)
Oddments of black and white for embroidery
1 pair of 3.25mm (UK10:US3) needles and a spare needle of same size for dungarees
Knitters' pins and a blunt-ended needle for sewing up
Acrylic toy stuffing
2 small buttons

FINISHED SIZE

Crocodile stands 6½in (16.5cm) tall

TENSION

26 sts x 34 rows measure 4in (10cm) square over st-st using 3.25mm needles and DK yarn before stuffing.

ABBREVIATIONS

See page 156

HOW TO MAKE CROCODILE

BODY AND HEAD

Using the long tail method and yarn A, cast on 36 sts.
Row 1: Purl.
Row 2: K1, (k8, m1, k1, m1, k8) twice, k1 (40 sts).
Rows 3 to 11: Beg with a p row, work 9 rows in st-st.
Rows 12 and 13: Work 2 rows in g-st to mark waist.
Row 14: Knit.
Row 15: K8, p24, k8.
Rows 16 to 23: Rep rows 14 and 15, 4 times more.
Row 24: K1, (k8, k3tog, k8) twice, k1 (36 sts).
Rows 25: K8, p20, k8.
Row 26: Knit.
Row 27: As row 25.
Row 28: K1, (k7, k3tog, k7) twice, k1 (32 sts).
Row 29: K8, p16, k8.
Row 30: Knit.
Rows 31 to 51: Rep rows 29 and 30, 10 times more, then row 29 once.
Row 52: K1, (k2tog, k2) to last 3 sts, k2tog, k1 (24 sts).
Row 53: K6, p12, K6.
Row 54: (K2tog) to end (12 sts).
Row 55: K3, p6, k3.
Break yarn and thread through sts on needle, pull tight and secure by threading yarn a second time through sts.

SNOUT

Using the long tail method and yarn A, cast on 26 sts.
Row 1: P9, k8, p9.
Row 2: Knit.
Row 3: As row 1.
Row 4: K7, k3tog, k6, k3tog, k7 (22 sts).
Row 5: P8, k6, p8.
Row 6: Knit.
Rows 7 to 15: Rep rows 5 and 6, 4 times more, then row 5 once.
Row 16: K5, k3tog, k6, k3tog, k5 (18 sts).
Row 17: P6, k6, p6.
Row 18: Knit.
Row 19: As row 17.
Row 20: K8, k2tog, k8 (17 sts).
Row 21: P6, k5, p6.
Row 22: Knit.
Row 23: As row 21.
Row 24: K3, k3tog, k5, k3tog, k3 (13 sts).
Rows 25 and 26: P 1 row then k 1 row.
Row 27: P3, p2tog, p3, p2tog, p3 (11 sts).
Cast off.

FEET AND LEGS (make 2)

Using the long tail method and yarn A, cast on 16 sts.
Row 1: Purl.
Row 2: (K1, kfb) 4 times, (kfb, k1) 4 times (24 sts).
Rows 3 to 7: Work 5 rows in st-st.
Row 8: K6, (k2tog) 6 times, k6 (18 sts).
Row 9: Purl.
Row 10: K7, (k2tog) twice, k7 (16 sts).
Rows 11 to 15: Work 5 rows in st-st.
Cast off.

HANDS AND FOREARMS (make 2)

Using the long tail method and yarn A, cast on 8 sts.
Row 1 and foll alt row: Purl.
Row 2: (Kfb) to end (16 sts).
Row 4: (Kfb, k1) to end (24 sts).
Rows 5 to 7: Work 3 rows in st-st.
Row 8: (K2tog) to end (12 sts).
Rows 9 to 15: Work 7 rows in st-st.
Row 16: (K2tog, k1) to end (8 sts).
Break yarn, thread through sts on needle and leave loose.

DUNGAREES (make 2 pieces)

Note: Foll individual instructions as given for 1 front and 1 back of dungarees.

First leg
Using the long tail method and yarn B, cast on 12 sts and beg in g-st.

Rows 1 and 2: Work 2 rows in g-st.
Break yarn and set aside.

Second leg
Work as for first leg but do not break yarn.

Join legs
Row 3: Beg with second leg and k10, k2tog, turn, using the knitting-on method cast on 5 sts, turn, then with the same yarn continue across first leg and k2tog, k to end (27 sts).
Row 4 and foll 2 alt rows: Purl.
Row 5: K2, m1, k23, m1, k2 (29 sts).
Row 7: K12, k2tog, k1, k2tog, k12 (27 sts).
Row 9: K10, k2tog, k3, k2tog, k10 (25 sts).
Rows 10 to 16: Work 7 rows in st-st.
Rows 17 to 19: Work 3 rows in g-st, ending with a RS row.
Cast off in g-st for back of dungarees or cont with bib for front of dungarees:

Divide for bib
Row 20: Cast off 6 sts kwise, k12 (13 sts now on RH needle), cast off rem 6 sts and fasten off.
Rejoin yarn to rem sts and patt:
Row 21: K2, (k1 tbl) 9 times, k2 (13 sts).
Row 22: K2, p9, k2.
Row 23: Knit.
Rows 24 to 29: Rep rows 22 and 23, 3 times more, ending with a k row.
Rows 30 and 31: Work 2 rows in g-st, ending with a RS row.
Cast off in g-st.

STRAPS FOR DUNGAREES (make 2)

Using the long tail method and yarn B, cast on 28 sts.
Row 1: Knit.
Cast off kwise.

TAIL

Using the long tail method and yarn A, cast on 22 sts.
Row 1: Purl.
Row 2: K3, (kfb) twice, k2, (kfb) twice, k4, (kfb) twice, k2, (kfb) twice, k3 (30 sts).
Rows 3 and 4: Work 2 rows in g-st ending with a RS row.
Row 5: P9, k12, p9.
Row 6: Knit
Rows 7 to 23: Rep rows 5 and 6, 8 times more, then row 5 once.
Row 24: K7, k3tog, k10, k3tog, k7 (26 sts).
Row 25: P8, k10, p8.
Row 26: Knit.
Rows 27 to 31: Rep rows 25 and 26 twice more, then row 25 once.
Row 32: K6, k3tog, k8, k3tog, k6 (22 sts).
Row 33: P7, k8, p7.
Row 34: Knit.
Rows 35 to 39: Rep rows 33 and 34 twice more, then row 33 once.
Row 40: K5, k3tog, k6, k3tog, k5 (18 sts).
Row 41: P6, k6, p6.
Row 42: Knit.
Row 43: As row 41.
Row 44: K8, k2tog, k8 (17 sts).
Row 45: P6, k5, p6.
Row 46: Knit.
Row 47: As row 45.
Row 48: K3, k3tog, k5, k3tog, k3 (13 sts).
Row 49: P4, k5, p4.
Row 50: Knit.
Row 51: P3, p2tog, p3, p2tog, p3 (11 sts).
Cast off.

MAKING UP

Note: Sew up all row-end seams on right side using mattress stitch one stitch in from the edge, unless otherwise stated; a one-stitch seam allowance has been allowed for this.

BODY AND HEAD

Sew up side edges of head and body leaving a gap. With this seam at centre back, oversew cast-on stitches. Stuff body and head and sew up gap.

SNOUT

Sew up side edges of snout and stuff. Pin and sew snout to head.

FEET AND LEGS

Fold cast-on stitches of feet in half and oversew. Sew up side edges of legs and stuff feet and legs. Pin legs to body, leaving a ¾in (2cm) gap at crotch, and sew in place.

HANDS AND FOREARMS

Gather round cast-on stitches of forearms, pull tight and secure. Sew up side edges of forearms and stuff. Pull stitches on a thread tight and secure. Sew forearms to Crocodile at both sides.

DUNGAREES, STRAPS AND BUTTONS

Make up dungarees, straps and buttons, as for Elephant on page 22.

TAIL

Sew up side edges of tail from tip to body and stuff. With seam at centre of underneath sew across cast-on stitches, then sew tail to Crocodile at back.

FEATURES

Mark position of eyes with two pins and embroider eyes in black making a vertical chain stitch for each eye then a second chain stitch on top of first. Embroider mouth in black using stem stitch and teeth in white using straight stitches (see page 155 for how to begin and fasten off invisibly for the embroidery).

VULTURE

INFORMATION YOU'LL NEED

MATERIALS

Any DK (US: light worsted) yarn (amounts given are approximate)
Yarn A dark brown (15g)
Yarn B mustard (10g)
Yarn C silver grey (5g)
Yarn D soft red (5g)
Yarn E petrol blue (10g)
Oddment of black for embroidery
1 pair of 3.25mm (UK10:US3) needles
Knitters' pins and a blunt-ended needle for sewing up
Tweezers (optional)
Acrylic toy stuffing
Thick cardboard
2 chenille stems
2 small buttons

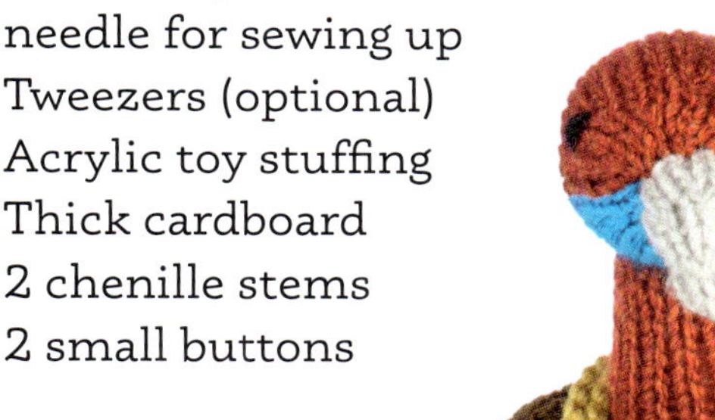

FINISHED SIZE

Vulture stands 8in (20.5cm) tall

TENSION

26 sts x 34 rows measure 4in (10cm) square over st-st using 3.25mm needles and DK yarn before stuffing.

ABBREVIATIONS

See page 156

SPECIAL ABBREVIATION

w1: wrap 1 stitch – take yarn between needles to opposite side, slip 1 stitch pwise from LH needle to RH needle, then take yarn between needles to first side.

HOW TO MAKE VULTURE

BODY

Using the long tail method and yarn A, cast on 8 sts.

Row 1 and foll 4 alt rows: Purl.

Row 2: (Kfb) to end (16 sts).

Row 4: (Kfb, k1) to end (24 sts).

Row 6: (Kfb, k2) to end (32 sts).

Row 8: (Kfb, k3) to end (40 sts).

Row 10: (Kfb, k4) to end (48 sts).

Rows 11 to 21: Work 11 rows in st-st.

Rows 22 and 23: Work 2 rows in g-st to mark waist.

Rows 24 to 27: Beg with a k row, work 4 rows in st-st.

Row 28: Cast off 5 sts at beg of next row, k37 (38 sts now on RH needle), cast off rem 5 sts and fasten off (38 sts).

Row 29: Rejoin yarn to rem sts and p 1 row.

Row 30: K2tog, k to last 2 sts, k2tog (36 sts).

Row 31: Purl.

Rows 32 to 35: Rep rows 30 and 31 twice more (32 sts).

Rows 36 and 37: Work 2 rows in st-st.

Row 38: (K2tog, k2) to end (24 sts).

Row 39 and foll alt row: Purl.

Row 40: (K2tog, k1) to end (16 sts).

Row 42: (K2tog) to end (8 sts).

Break yarn and thread through sts on needle, pull tight and secure by threading yarn a second time through sts.

DUNGAREES

Using the long tail method and yarn B, cast on 8 sts.

Row 1 and foll 5 alt rows: Purl.

Row 2: (Kfb) to end (16 sts).

Row 4: (Kfb) to end (32 sts).

Row 6: (Kfb, k3) to end (40 sts).

Row 8: (Kfb, k4) to end (48 sts).

Row 10: (Kfb, k5) to end (56 sts).

Row 12: (Kfb, k6) to end (64 sts).

Rows 13 to 23: Beg with a p row, work 11 rows in st-st.

Rows 24 to 26: Work 3 rows in g-st, ending with a RS row.

Divide for bib

Row 27: Cast off 25 sts kwise, k13 (14 sts now on RH needle), cast off rem 25 sts kwise and fasten off.

Re-join yarn to rem sts and patt:

Row 28: K2, (k1 tbl) 10 times, k2 (14 sts).

Row 29: K2, p10, k2.

Row 30: Knit.

Rows 31 to 34: Rep rows 29 and 30 twice more, ending with a k row.

Rows 35 and 36: Work 2 rows in g-st ending with a RS row.

Cast off in g-st.

LEGS (make 2)

Using the long tail method and yarn C, cast on 7 sts.

Row 1: Purl.

Row 2: (Kfb) to end (14 sts).

Rows 3 to 7: Work 5 rows in st-st.

Row 8: Change to yarn B and k 1 row.

Row 9: K4, (kfb, k4) twice (16 sts).

Rows 10 to 13: Beg with a k row, work 4 rows in st-st.

Cast off.

FEET, BACK TOE AND TOES (make 2)

Make feet, back toe and toes using yarn C, as for Weaver Bird on page 85.

NECK

Using the long tail method and yarn D, cast on 16 sts.

Rows 1 to 3: Beg with a p row, work 3 rows in st-st.

Row 4: K12, w1, turn.

Row 5: S1p, p8, w1, turn.

Row 6: S1k, k to end.

Rows 7 to 12: Rep rows 1 to 6 once.

Row 13: Purl.

Row 14: K5, w1, turn.

Row 15: S1p, p to end.

Row 16: Knit.

Row 17: P5, w1, turn.

Row 18: S1k, k to end.

Cast off pwise.

HEAD

Using the long tail method and yarn D, cast on 6 sts.

Row 1 and foll alt row: Purl.

Row 2: (Kfb) to end (12 sts).

Row 4: (Kfb) to end (24 sts).

Rows 5 to 7: Work 3 rows in st-st. Join on yarn E and work in yarn D and E in intarsia, twisting yarn when changing colour to avoid a hole.
Row 8: Yarn D-k14, yarn E-k10.
Row 9: Yarn E-p10, yarn D-p14.
Rows 10 to 15: Rep rows 8 and 9, 3 times more.
Row 16: Yarn D-k2, (k2tog, k2) 3 times, yarn E-k1, (k2tog, k1) 3 times more (18 sts).
Row 17: Yarn E-p7, yarn D-p11.
Row 18: Yarn D-k2tog, (k1, k2tog) 3 times, yarn E-k1, (k2tog, k1) twice (12 sts).
Row 19: Yarn E-p5, yarn D-p7.
Break yarn and thread through sts on needle, pull tight and secure by threading yarn a second time through sts.

BEAK

Using the long tail method and yarn C, cast on 12 sts.
Rows 1 to 3: Beg with a p row, work 3 rows in st-st.
Row 4: K2, (k2tog) 4 times, k2 (8 sts).
Rows 5 and 6: P 1 row then k 1 row.
Row 7: P2, (p2tog) twice, p2 (6 sts).
Rows 8 and 9: K 1 row then p 1 row.
Break yarn and thread through sts on needle, pull tight and secure by threading yarn a second time through sts.

TAIL

Using the two-needle method and yarn A, cast on 15 sts and work in g-st.
Rows 1 to 4: Work 4 rows in g-st.
Row 5: Cast off 10 sts, kfb, k3 (6 sts).
Row 6: Knit.
Row 7: Cast on 12 sts using the knitting-on method at beg of next row and k this row (18 sts).
Rows 8 to 10: Work 3 rows in g-st.
Row 11: Cast off 13 sts, kfb, k3 (6 sts).
Row 12: Knit.
Row 13: Cast on 9 sts using the knitting-on method at beg of next row and k this row (15 sts).
Rows 14 to 16: Work 3 rows in g-st.
Cast off in g-st.

WINGS (make 2)

Using the two-needle method and yarn A, cast on 13 sts and work in g-st.
Row 1: Knit.
Row 2: Kfb, k10, k2tog.
Row 3: Knit.
Row 4: As row 2.
Row 5: Cast off 5 sts, kfb, k5, kfb (10 sts).
Row 6: Kfb, k7, k2tog.
Row 7: Cast on 5 sts using the knitting-on method at beg of next row and k this row (15 sts).
Row 8: Kfb, k12, k2tog.
Row 9: Knit.
Row 10: As row 8.
Row 11: Cast off 5 sts, kfb, k7, kfb (12 sts).
Row 12: Kfb, k9, k2tog.
Row 13: Cast on 5 sts using the knitting-on method at beg of next row and k this row (17 sts).
Row 14: Kfb, k14, k2tog.
Row 15: Knit.
Row 16: As row 14.
Row 17: Cast off 5 sts, kfb, k9, kfb (14 sts).
Row 18: Knit.
Row 19: Cast on 12 sts at beg of next row and k this row (26 sts).
Rows 20 to 22: Work 3 rows in g-st.
Cast off in g-st.

STRAPS (make 2)

Using the long tail method and yarn B, cast on 22 sts.
Row 1: Knit.
Cast off kwise.

MAKING UP

Note: Sew up all row-end seams on right side using mattress stitch one stitch in from the edge, unless otherwise stated; a one-stitch seam allowance has been allowed for this.

BODY AND HEAD

Gather round cast-on stitches of body, pull tight and secure. Sew up side edges and cast-off stitches of back leaving a gap, stuff and sew up gap.

DUNGAREES

Sew up side edges of dungarees and place on Vulture. Sew cast-off stitches of dungarees to waist of body using back stitch.

LEGS

Sew up side edges of legs and stuff legs. Sew legs to underneath of Vulture sewing through dungarees to body.

FEET AND TOES

Sew up side edges of back toe of foot and stuff back toe with a tiny bit of stuffing with tweezers or tip of scissors. Finish sewing up side edges and place inside a triangle of thick cardboard measuring 1in (2.5cm) on narrow edge and 1¼in (3cm) on tall sides. Oversew cast-on stitches enclosing cardboard inside. Sew up side edges of each toe and sew a toe to middle of each foot and two more either side at front. Sew feet to ends of legs.

NECK

Sew up side edges of neck. Take 2 chenille stems placed together and fold in half. Put chenille stems inside neck, then stuff neck. Cut excess chenille stem and sew lower edge of neck to body.

HEAD

Sew up side edges of head leaving a gap, stuff and sew up gap. Pin and sew head to top of neck.

BEAK

Sew up side edges of beak and pull this seam tight to curve beak. Stuff beak with tweezers or tip of scissors and pin and sew beak to head.

TAIL AND WINGS

Sew tail to back of body. Sew wings to Vulture at each side.

STRAPS AND BUTTONS

Sew straps to each side of bib, take straps over back, cross over and sew ends of straps to top of dungarees. Add two buttons to bib.

FEATURES

Mark position of eyes with two pins and embroider eyes in black making a chain stitch for each eye and a second chain stitch on top of first (see page 155 for how to begin and fasten off invisibly for the embroidery).

TECHNIQUES

GETTING STARTED

BUYING YARN

The patterns for the designs in this book are worked in double knitting (or light worsted in the US). There are many yarns on the market, from natural fibres to acrylic blends. Acrylic yarn is a good choice as it washes without shrinking, but always follow the care instructions on the ball band. Be cautious about using a brushed or mohair-type yarn if the toy is intended for a baby or a very young child, as the fibres can be swallowed.

SAFETY ADVICE

Some of the toys have small pieces and trimmings, which could present a choking hazard. Make sure that small parts are sewn down securely before giving any of the toys to a baby or young child.

TENSION

All the toys in this book are knitted on 3.25mm (UK10:US3) knitting needles. This should turn out at approximately 26 stitches and 34 rows over 4in (10cm) square. If there are fewer stitches, the stuffing might show through the fabric and look unsightly. If you use smaller needles the knitting will become tighter.

SLIP KNOT

1. Wind the yarn from the ball round your left index finger from front to back and then to front again. Slide the loop from your finger and pull the new loop through from the centre. Place this loop from back to front onto the needle that is in your right hand.

2. Pull the tail of yarn down to tighten the knot slightly and pull the yarn from the ball to form a loose knot.

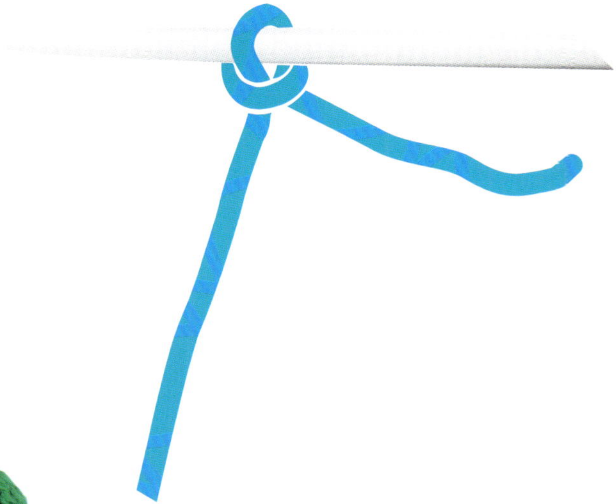

CASTING ON

(using the long tail method)

1. Leave a long length of yarn: as a rough guide, allow ⅜in (1cm) for each stitch to be cast on plus an extra length for sewing up. Make a slip knot.

2. Hold the needle in your right hand with your index finger on the slip knot loop to keep it in place. Wrap the loose tail end round your left thumb, from front to back. Push the needle's point through the thumb loop from front to back. Wind the ball end of the yarn round the needle from left to right.

3. Pull the loop through the thumb loop, then remove your thumb. Gently pull the new loop tight using the tail yarn.

Repeat this process until the required number of stitches are on the needle.

KNITTING STITCHES

KNIT STITCH

1. Hold needle with stitches in left hand. Hold yarn at back of work and insert point of right-hand empty needle into the front loop of the first stitch. Wrap yarn around point of right-hand needle in a clockwise direction using your index finger.

2. With yarn still wrapped around the point, bring the right-hand needle back towards you through the loop of the first stitch. Try to keep the free yarn fairly taut but not too slack or tight.

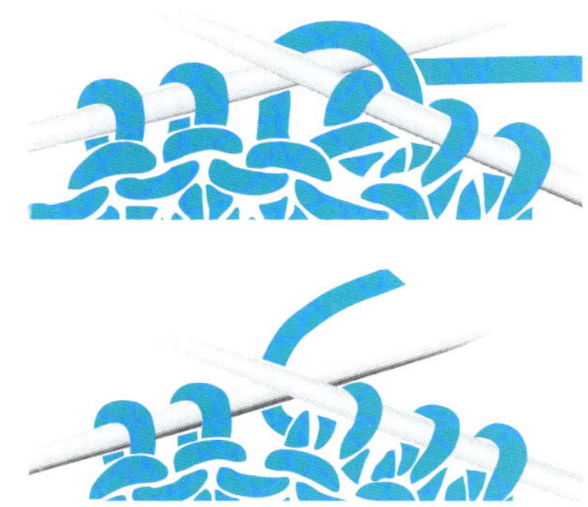

3. Finally, with the new stitch firmly on the right-hand needle, gently pull the old stitch to the right and off the tip of the left-hand needle. Repeat for all the knit stitches across the row.

PURL STITCH

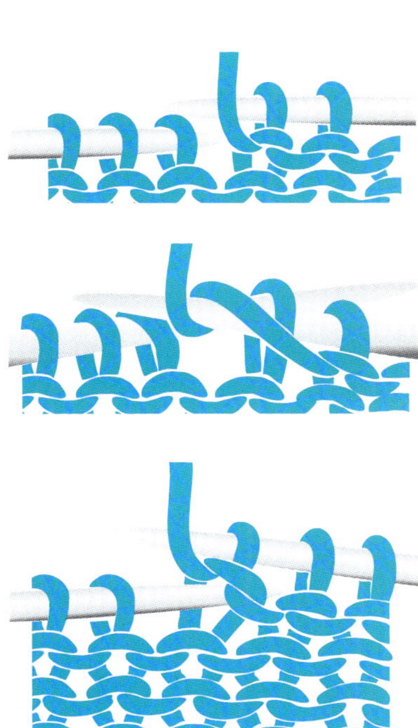

1. Hold needles with stitches in left hand and hold yarn at front of work.

2. Insert point of right-hand empty needle into the front loop of the first stitch. Wrap yarn around point of right-hand needle in an anticlockwise direction using index finger. Bring yarn back to front of work.

3. Now with yarn still wrapped around point of right-hand needle, bring it back through the stitch. Try to keep free yarn taut but not too slack or tight. Finally, with the new stitch firmly on the right-hand needle, gently pull the old stitch off the tip of the left-hand needle. Repeat for all the purl stitches along the row.

GARTER STITCH (A)

This is made by knitting every row.

STOCKING STITCH (B)

Probably the most commonly used stitch in knitting, this is created by knitting on the right side and purling on the wrong side.

REVERSE STOCKING STITCH (C)

This is made in the same way as stocking stitch but the reverse side is the right side.

RIB STITCH (D)

This is made by knitting the first stitch, then bringing the yarn between the needles to front of knitting and purling the next stitch. Take the yarn back and continue knitting then purling alternately along row. On the next row, knit all stitches that were purled on the previous row and purl all stitches that were knitted on the previous row.

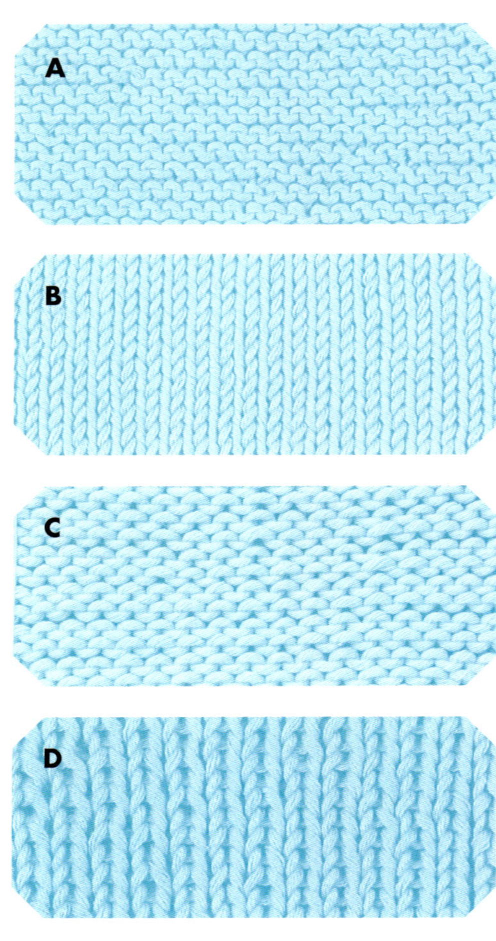

SHAPING

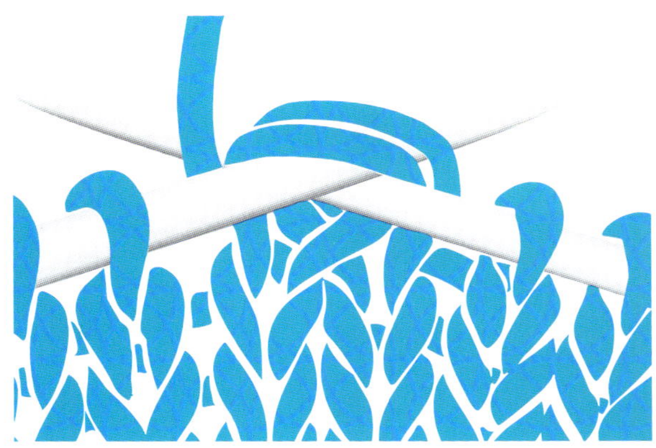

DECREASING

To decrease a stitch, when instructed k2tog or p2tog, simply work two stitches together to make one stitch out of the two stitches. Or if the instructions say k3tog or p3tog, then work three stitches together to make one out of the three.

To achieve a neat appearance to your finished work, this is done as follows:

At the beginning of a knit row and throughout the row, k2tog by knitting two stitches together through the front of the loops (as shown above).

At the end of a knit row, if these are the very last two stitches in the row, then knit together through the back of the loops.

At the beginning of a purl row, if these are the very first stitches in the row, then purl together through the back of the loops. Purl two together along the rest of the row through the front of the loops.

INCREASING

Two methods are used in this book for increasing the number of stitches: m1 and kfb.

M1 Make a stitch by picking up the horizontal loop between the needles and placing it onto the left-hand needle. Now knit into the back of it to twist it on a knit row, or purl into the back of it on a purl row.

Kfb or pfb Make a stitch on a knit row by knitting into the front then back of the next stitch. To do this, simply knit into the next stitch but do not slip it off. Take the point of the right-hand needle around and knit again into the back of the stitch before removing the loop from the left-hand needle. You now have made two stitches out of one.

KNITTING ON STITCHES

(or two-needle casting on)

1. Insert the right-hand needle from front to back between the first and second stitches on the left-hand needle and wrap the yarn around the tip of the right-hand needle from back to front.

2. Slide the right-hand needle through to the front to catch the new loop of yarn.

3. Place the new loop of yarn onto the left-hand needle, inserting the left-hand needle from front to back. Repeat this process until you have reached the required number of cast-on stitches.

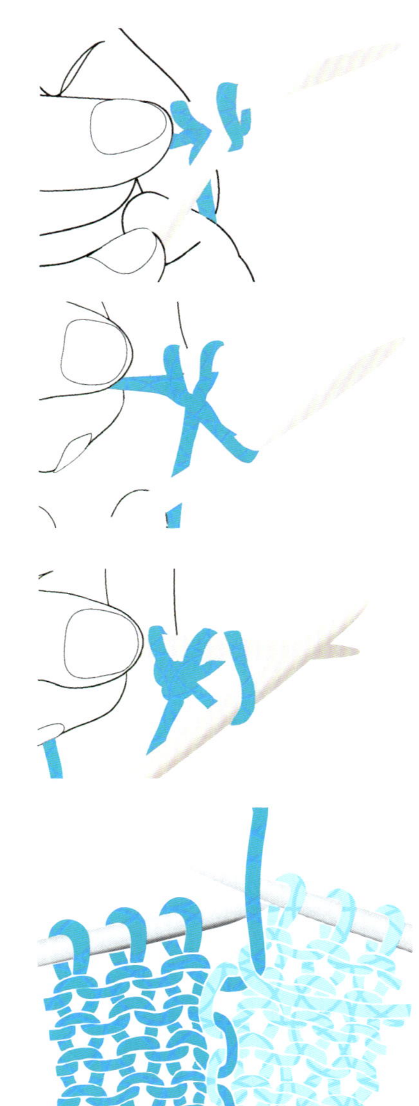

INTARSIA

Blocks of colour are worked using the intarsia technique. Twist the two different yarns together at the back of the work with each colour change to prevent holes appearing. Once finished, weave in ends at the back of the work.

CASTING OFF

1. Knit two stitches onto the right-hand needle, then slip the first stitch over the second and let it drop off the needle. One stitch remains on the needle.

2. Knit another stitch so you have two stitches on the right-hand needle again.

Repeat the process until only one stitch is left on the left-hand needle. Break the yarn, thread it through the remaining stitch and pull tight to fasten off.

SPECIAL INSTRUCTIONS

THREADING YARN THROUGH STITCHES

Sometimes the instructions will tell you to 'thread yarn through stitches on needle, pull tight and secure'. To do this, first break the yarn, leaving a long end, and thread a blunt-ended sewing needle with this end. Pass the needle through all the stitches on the knitting needle, slipping each stitch off the knitting needle in turn. Draw the yarn through the stitches. To secure, pass the needle once again through all the stitches in a complete circle and pull tight.

MAKING-UP INSTRUCTIONS

MATTRESS STITCH (A)

Join row ends by taking small straight stitches back and forth on the right side of work, one stitch from the edge.

OVERSEWING (B)

Pieces can also be joined by oversewing on the wrong side and turning the piece right side out. For smaller pieces or pieces that cannot be turned, oversew on the right side.

BACK STITCH (C)

Bring needle out at the beginning of the stitch line, make a small stitch and bring the needle out slightly further along the stitch line. Insert the needle at the end of the first stitch and bring it out still further along the stitch line. Continue in the same way to create a line of joined stitches.

STUFFING AND AFTERCARE

Spend a little time stuffing your knitted toy evenly. Acrylic toy stuffing is ideal for this; make sure to use plenty, but not so much that it stretches the knitted fabric so the stuffing can be seen through the stitches. Tweezers are useful for stuffing small parts.

Washable filling is recommended for all the stuffed toys so that you can hand-wash them with a non-biological detergent. Do not spin or tumble dry, but gently squeeze the excess water out, arrange the toy into its original shape, and leave it to dry.

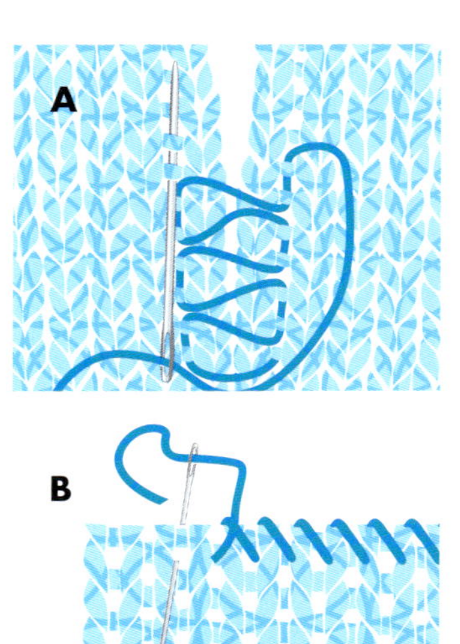

FINISHING TOUCHES

EMBROIDERY

To begin embroidery invisibly, tie a knot in the end of the yarn. Take a large stitch through the work, coming up to begin the embroidery. Allow the knot to disappear through the knitting and be caught in the stuffing. To fasten off invisibly, sew a few stitches back and forth through the work, inserting the needle where the yarn comes out.

CHAIN STITCH

Bring the needle up through your work to start the first stitch and hold down the thread with the left thumb. Now insert the needle in the same place and bring the point out a short distance away. Keeping the working thread under the needle point, pull the loop of thread to form a chain.

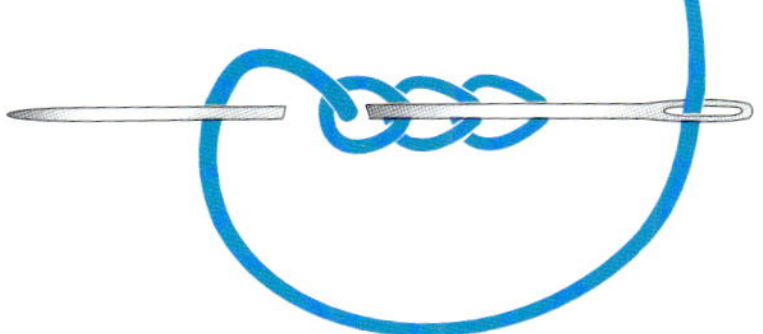

STEM STITCH

Starting at the left-hand side and working towards the right-hand side, work small stitches backwards along the stitch line with the thread always emerging on the same side of the previous stitch.

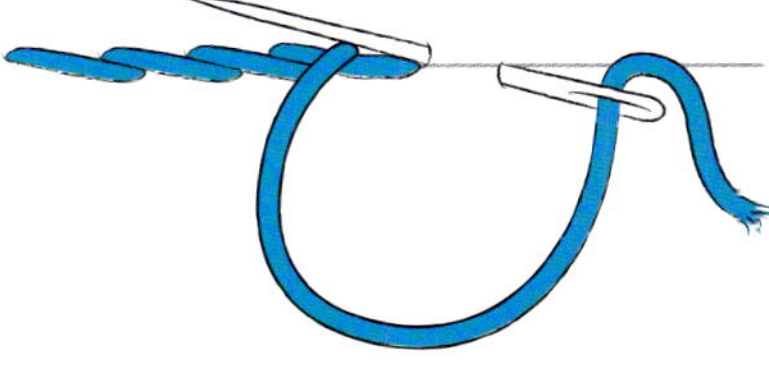

STRAIGHT STITCH

Come up to start the embroidery at one end of the stitch then go back down at the end of the stitch, coming up in a different place to start the next stitch.

SATIN STITCH

Work a series of straight stitches closely together.

ABBREVIATIONS

alt	alternate
approx	approximately
beg	beginning
cm	centimetre(s)
cont	continue
dec	decrease/decreasing
DK	double knitting
foll	following
g-st	garter stitch: knit every row
g	gram(s)
inc	increase/increasing
k	knit/knitting
k2tog or k3tog	knit two or three stitches together: if these are the very last row, then work through back of loops
kfb	make two stitches out of one: knit into the front then the back of the next stitch
kwise	knitwise
LH	left hand
m1	make one stitch: pick up horizontal loop between the needles and work into the back of it to twist it
mm	millimetre(s)
p	purl
p2tog or p3tog	purl two or three stitches together: if these stitches are the very first in the row, then work together through back of loops
pfb	make two stitches out of one: purl into the front then the back of next stitch
patt	pattern
pwise	purlwise
rem	remaining
rep	repeat(ed)
rev st-st	reverse stocking stitch: purl on the right side, knit on the wrong side
RH	right hand
RS	right side
s1k	slip one stitch knitwise
s1p	slip one stitch purlwise
st(s)	stitch(es)
st-st	stocking stitch: knit on the right side, purl on the wrong side
tbl	through back of loop(s)
tog	together
WS	wrong side
Yf	yarn forward
( )	repeat instructions between brackets as many times as instructed
*** or ****	repeat from * or ** as instructed

CONVERSIONS

KNITTING NEEDLES

UK	Metric	US
10	3.25mm	3

YARN WEIGHT

UK	US
Double knitting	Light worsted

TERMINOLOGY

UK	US
Cast off	Bind off
Stocking stitch	Stockinette stitch
Tension	Gauge
Anticlockwise	Counterclockwise

INDEX

ACKNOWLEDGEMENTS

Thank you to GMC for making this book possible, and to friends and family for their enthusiasm and encouragement. And thank you to Cynthia and Helen, from my local Wool Shop (www.clarewools.co.uk), who provided the materials and were extremely enthusiastic every step of the way.

DEDICATED TO

Cheryl Caldwell

First published 2025 by
Guild of Master Craftsman Publications Ltd,
Castle Place, 166 High Street, Lewes, East Sussex,
BN7 1XU, UK
www.gmcbooks.com

ISBN 978 1 78494 715 6

The EEA authorised representative is Authorised Rep Compliance Ltd. Ground Floor, 71 Baggot Street Lower, Dublin, DO2 P593, Ireland
www.arccompliance.com

A catalogue record for this book is available from the British Library.

Publisher Jonathan Bailey
Production Jim Bulley
Senior Project Editor Sara Harper
Pattern Checker Jude Roust
Design Manager Robin Shields
Designer Hanri Van Wyk
Photography Andrew Perris

Colour origination by GMC Reprographics
Printed and bound in China

To order a book, contact:
GMC Publications Ltd
Castle Place, 166 High Street,
Lewes, East Sussex, BN7 1XU,
United Kingdom
Tel: +44 (0)1273 488005
www.gmcbooks.com